The First-Time Parent's Survival Guide

Presents a clear unvarnished vision of what having a
baby really means.

D0532940

$2

The
First-Time
Parent's
Survival Guide

**Tells the whole truth about pregnancy
and parenthood with practical tips to
enable you to enjoy both**

by

CAROL HOWLAND

Illustrated by Linda North

THORSONS PUBLISHING GROUP
Wellingborough · New York

First published 1986

© CAROL HOWLAND 1986

British Library Cataloguing in Publication Data

Howland, Carol
    The first time parent's survival guide: tells
    the whole truth about pregnancy and
    parenthood with practical tips to enable
    you to enjoy both
    1. Parenthood
    I. Title
    306.8'74   HQ755.8
    ISBN 0-7225-1276-7

Printed and bound in Great Britain

Contents

	Page
Introduction	7
Chapter	

PART I: MOTHERHOOD AND YOU

1. Mum's the Word	13
2. You and Your Job	18
3. Financial Changes	26
4. Single Parenthood	35
5. Baby-Bashing — Am I the Sort Who Might?	38
6. Babies — How They Differ	43
7. Changing Relationships	47

PART II: FIRST BABY - YEAR ONE

8. Preparing for the Siege	77
9. The Emotional Everest	84
10. How Fathers Can Help	90
11. The First Four Months	95
12. From Solid Food to Crawling	109
13. Another Baby Now?	116
14. Crawling to Walking	121
15. End of Year Assessment	126

PART III: YEAR TWO AND BEYOND

16. Toddling	133
17. Talking	139
18. The Second Child	146
19. Travelling with Children	155

20. Conclusion   168

   Bibliography   171
   Useful Addresses   172
   Index   173

Introduction

In the 1970s, women's pleas were for equal pay, maternity leave and job protection so that they could more easily combine motherhood and careers. It is still not easy. Day nurseries geared to the working mother remain rare, and many young women, possibly for the first time in history, are taking a long and less emotional look at whether or not to have children at all.

The idea for this book came as a result of conversations I had with several single friends who were vaguely yearning for marriage and motherhood, but who had no idea of how it would affect their lifestyles. The object of the book is to present prospective parents with a clear, unvarnished vision of what having a family means: to help them to make the decision whether or not to start a family, and to help those who are already expecting a child to prepare for the many adjustments that lie ahead. I hope also that it will serve to soothe the guilt of those who are already struggling through the throes of parenthood who feel a bit of a failure because they are unable to live up to the warm, glowing images of parenthood. For surely, there is something a little bit wrong, or at least incomplete, in those images, and therefore, with our dreams and expectations. Well, we haven't been told the whole truth.

The question I want to answer is: if anyone knew what having children was really like, would they have them?

This book could have been written by any contemporary mother. I say contemporary because it is only recently that we have begun to be brave enough to look the sacred cow of motherhood squarely in the face. Until the Pill, women had babies because it was difficult to avoid having them. With the arrival of the Pill, women began to plan *when* they would have their babies. It is only in the very recent past that a few women have started to question whether or not to have children at all, although most of us go on reproducing without giving it much thought.

Becoming a mother, sometime, is still very much a part of our cultural heritage. Nearly everyone does it, and parents, friends and workmates expect it of us. Adding their voices to those of our nearest and dearest, manufacturers of baby foods, toys, clothes and nursery furniture, the newspapers, radio, television and women's magazines tout glamourized images of mothers and babies. The pressures of society still push us firmly towards being fruitful and multiplying. Even in the 1980s, despite two decades of fairly reliable contraception, it is still a courageous woman who stands up to her lover or husband, to his parents and hers, and announces that she does not intend having a family.

The trouble with making the decision of whether or not to have a baby is that it must be made without prior knowledge of what motherhood is really like. No one can tell you how *you* are going to feel about becoming a mother until you are one. Even if you have worked as a nurse, taught in a nursery or an infant school, had lots of younger brothers or sisters, or looked after someone else's children, even for long periods on a regular basis, it is not the same as having children of your own. To be sure, you would have a head start on someone like me, who as an only child had no experience of young children at all. But it seems ironic that probably the most important decisions of our lives — what jobs we will train for, who we will marry, whether or not to have children — must be taken from a position of relative ignorance.

This book is an attempt, in some small measure, to let you inside the experience of motherhood to prepare you for what it is really like. Most 'baby books' dwell on the rosy-hued joys of motherhood — and, of course, there are joys — but my object is to cut through the rosy haze and to look at the nuts-and-bolts reality, too.

I have therefore made very little effort to balance the negative aspects of motherhood with winsome memories to touch your emotions. That doesn't mean to say that motherhood to me, necessarily, is negative — not at all — but simply that the positive side is so overly exposed everywhere else that I have tried for the most part to keep my attention to what, up to now, the other 'baby books' do not discuss, i.e. how motherhood is going to affect a woman's daily life.

If this puts you off motherhood, so be it. It is better that you know what motherhood is like before it hits you. If it doesn't put you off, I only hope that it will give you enough foresight to avoid the shock that motherhood often is, and will enable you to cope better than you might have done otherwise. And for those readers who already have children, I hope that it will serve as a soothing balm and make you realize that you are not alone.

Bookshops and libraries are full of books describing the various stages of pregnancy and birth, along with a bewildering choice of books on how to bring up babies and young children. For this reason, I will not go over this well-beaten path more than is absolutely unavoidable. Out of the dozen or so books that I devoured when I was first pregnant, only one (*Hard Labour* by Jean and John Lennane, a husband and wife team, both doctors, published by Victor Gollancz, 1977) gave any inkling of what it would be like as a new mother with a newborn baby.

Thanks to the Lennanes' warnings, advice, and warm-hearted support, I staggered through the night feeds, if not sailing, at least knowing that it was perfectly normal to feel as I did. The floundering did not set in until the baby reached the crawling stage, and there seemed to be no book to turn to. I felt utterly frustrated, isolated, and guilty at feeling frustrated — worse, a failure at what I most wanted to be good at, being the best mother I possibly could. If only someone had written a book that went a bit further. No one seems to have done it, so here goes.

PART I:
Motherhood and You

1. Mum's The Word

Months before my husband and I were getting married, we discussed whether or not to have children. I would only consider having children, I proclaimed, if he really wanted them, and if he were willing to be a truly participating father. I'm sure you have heard that term, 'participating father'. What I, in my innocence, did not go on to discuss with him was just how 'participating' participating was to be.

Now, with hindsight, I realize that there are shades of 'participating', which can vary greatly. They range from the reverse-role father, who takes over completely while his wife goes back to her career; the father who does a split shift with his wife, so that they can both hold down part-time jobs; the father who continues in his full-time job, but who takes the baby or children off his wife's hands at the weekends so that she can have a break; the father who shares the child-minding chores with his wife whenever he is at home; the father who will sometimes get up at night to find out why the baby is crying; or, as one of my friends rather acidly put it, 'The father who is *not too disturbed* when his wife has to get up a couple of times a night to feed the baby.' I assure you, they all exist.

Psychologists say that whether or not we like or approve of how our parents brought us up, we tend to repeat the style of it (unless we over-compensate in the opposite direction); so it is wise to compare childhoods with your partner to iron out areas of disagreement, to air your expectations of him as a father, and to find out what he expects of you as a mother. Starting with basics, it is you, the woman, who will become pregnant and who must suffer any of the sickness, aches, pains and inconveniences. It is you, the woman, who must bear the child, hopefully with the loving moral support of your husband. Thereafter, the choices begin, or so we think.

I maintain that women are sabotaged from within. No matter how hard a woman may try to carry on her life as before, it does not happen that way. Regardless of who or what she may have been up to the instant that her baby is born, a woman takes on a whole new — additional — role. So does a man, you might say, but bear with me. If you decide to have children, you must realize that it is most probably *you*, the woman, who will shoulder most of the responsibility for looking after first the babies, and later the toddlers, during the early, most demanding years of their lives. *Your total existence that will become dominated by child care!*

The sabotage is triggered like this. When you become pregnant, it is you who must eat the right things, not gain too much weight, look out for high blood-pressure — you are *already* in charge of the unborn baby's welfare. It is most likely you who will decide whether to bottle or breast-feed your baby. If you have a job to which you plan to return, although you and your husband may make the decision together about how the baby will be looked after, it will almost certainly be *you* who will have to do the arranging: finding a day nursery, a nanny or a child minder, and *you* who will be expected to stay at home from your job if the baby becomes ill!

If you decide to breast-feed, the 'participating' dad is rather neatly cut out of the feeding scene. He can learn to change, dress and bathe the baby along with you. He can take the baby out in the pram for walks. But *you* have always got to be somewhere not too far away in case the baby gets hungry. So even *before* the baby is born, it is the mother who tends to make the decisions concerning the baby's welfare, and after, about how the baby will be cared for, even if she doesn't do it herself! *She* becomes responsible.

If a woman breast-feeds, she must fulfill one of the baby's most urgent needs — feeding. Because babies let us know that they are hungry by crying, whenever a baby cries, those around him assume that he might well be hungry. This can all too easily be extended to the mother having to go to see if the baby wants the breast, whenever the baby cries. The result is that the mother is on first call. It is a very rare father who, upon hearing his newborn baby cry, thinks to suggest that *he* might go and see if the baby needs changing, if the baby would like to be picked up, if he needs to be tilted in his cot to get rid of hiccups, or anything else, even in the daytime, if the father is there. But five days out of seven, usually he isn't there. At night, fathers seldom even wake up. The baby cries; the mother goes.

There is a case to be made, I suppose, that it's instinct. The sound of a tiny newborn baby crying is very distressing to anyone listening, and intensely so to the baby's mother, who somehow feels that she ought to be able to help. It used to cut me like a knife, and I have heard of lactating mothers feeling the milk 'go down' in their breasts upon hearing a baby cry, even though it wasn't their own baby.

With repetition — the baby cries, the mother goes — the pattern quickly becomes reinforced into habit. It doesn't take long for the baby to become solely the mother's responsibility unless the father is extremely eager, determined, and encouraged. The trouble is that, eager and determined though he may be, most fathers simply are not there during a large part of the baby's life.

As I said before, even if you return to your job when the baby is a few weeks old, as the mother, the responsibility both for organizing the baby's care and looking after him when you are at home will almost inevitably fall to you. Very rarely do circumstances free a mother from the necessity of being constantly on call, round the clock, week in and week out, from the moment the baby is born until whenever young children stop waking in the night, frightened of the dark or a scary nightmare. With a newborn baby this means always having an ear cocked in the direction of the baby's room to hear that first cry, and as the baby becomes older and mobile, *watching his every waking move* to keep him from harm.

It's very odd that although fathers *think* they feel a sense of responsibility for their offspring, they are never — with perhaps the exception of reverse-role fathers, who stay at home to look after their children while their wives go back to work — tuned in to *anticipate* how a child can hurt himself. Every mother I have talked to says the same. Fathers are simply not on the same wavelength. Even if a mother asks her husband to watch the children, she has to explain in great detail all of the hazards that *might* come up in the course of the father's watching, because the father will not recognize the possible dangers until too late.

I know that sounds damning, but I remember sitting on a beach, saying to my husband, 'Now I'd like to lie down and close my eyes for a few minutes. Will you please keep an eye on her, and go after her if she gets more than ten yards away.' Or when going out to the garden, 'Don't let her out of your sight for an instant or she could easily fall down those stone steps.' Once, when I was heavily pregnant and unable to spring out of a lawnchair quickly, I said, 'Look, she's going up those stairs. Please go after her *now*, because she won't be able to come back down.' He didn't leap, she wasn't able to reach the handrail and she took a three-step tumble bashing her forehead on the concrete below.

I'm sure this sixth sense of impending disaster, or possible disaster, develops because it is usually the mother, having close daily contact with the child, who has a very good measure of exactly what the child is and is not capable of. Fathers, who often don't see their babies from one weekend to the next, cannot possibly have their fingertips on the pulse of development to the same extent. What I find strange is that the fathers don't seem to feel that inner sense of personal responsibility for their own children that mothers feel. Unless a father is asked nicely to take charge, he doesn't think to do so. He just lets the mother get on with it — an outgrowth, I suspect, of the breast-feeding pattern when the mother must answer one of the baby's primary needs.

Bottle feeding, in theory, should be different. Either parent can just as well prepare the formula and give the baby a bottle. But in practice, unless the mother has hired a nanny or a child-minder (or found a day nursery) or the father has opted to stay at home to look after the baby while she goes back to work, the motherly duties will settle upon her within the first few days at home from the maternity hospital with greater or lesser, usually lesser, assistance from dad.

This is not meant to be unkind or ungenerous to fathers. But just look at the facts. Whether or not a woman goes back to a job when the baby is a few weeks or a few months old, she is the parent having sole charge of the baby during his first few days of life in the maternity ward, then she comes home and looks after the baby, with or without help *until she returns to her job*, if she returns to her job. The father continues in his job, usually without interruption, unless he takes some time off to help his wife out when she comes home — and what better way for both parents to begin this new adventure of parenthood, than together?

Once the father returns to his job with its schedules and pressures after 'paternity leave,' he comes home at night looking forward to putting his feet up and a good meal. The mother 'naturally' — unless she has hired a nanny or child-minder — takes over caring for the baby during the day. But the idea that the mother of a newborn baby is *not working* at home, looking after a baby, must be dispelled, the sooner the better. She is probably working far harder at the most emotionally and physically demanding job she will ever have!

Obviously, women recover from childbirth after varying lengths of time, depending upon the duration of the labour, whether or not it was a Caesarean birth, and whether the birth meant losing a night's sleep, or more. Some of the necessary rest may be recouped in the maternity hospital (provided the baby, or the one in the cot beside hers, doesn't cry too often in the night). So it is foolish to rush home with a new baby. But even after those first few desperate, doggedly tired days, it can be weeks — usually until the baby starts sleeping through the night — before a mother can really begin to regain her strength.

I remember my dismay when a friend warned me that she hadn't really 'felt herself' until at least a year after the birth of her baby. In some ways, I had certainly recovered long before then, but looking back, I must admit that there were other ways in which I hadn't. I only wish she had told me why, and in what ways. I shall endeavour to do so in the chapters to follow.

2. You and Your Job

Some women view getting pregnant as the great escape from a dull or otherwise unsatisfying job. But hold it a minute until you have had a good close look at all the implications — despite its sweet moments.

> To cuddle this newborn child brought such profound bliss, not only emotional, but in small physical pleasures. The touch of her skin was like rose petals, the fine fluff on her head softer than velvet. The sight of her curved forehead, her dimpled double chin and her plump toes always made me smile; she plucked my heartstrings when she curled her tiny fingers tightly around one of mine. To hold her, to stroke her, to hug her gently were pure joy. Although the desire to have a child had come rather late in life, with my arms wrapped around this tiny, warm lump of love, I felt, strangely, that before, my arms had always been empty. [Written a few months after the birth of our first child.]

But along with the sweet moments, motherhood can also be an extremely dull job with no escape once you've made the decision. The hours are long, twelve to eighteen a day if you're lucky, with rare tea breaks (except during the first year or two while the baby naps), seven days a week, month after month, year after year. There are no weekends, no holidays, no pay, no overtime, and a reduced standard of living to boot!

This is not to put you off, but it is only fair to warn you that the tedium of motherhood, along with the joys, can be intense, the frustration at not being able to do some of the things *you* want to do exasperating, if not downright depressing, with not many compensating feelings of accomplishment, success, or even the satisfaction of completing a task or a project. Certainly there are the joys of holding and cuddling your smiling baby, the joys of watching his first efforts to grasp a ball, to roll over unaided, to sit up and later to crawl and to walk. There are the delights of watching his daily progress in learning to get a spoon to his mouth, to bounce in his bouncing chair, and to scoot along in a baby walker. But these are *his* achievements.

A mother's success is when after weeks or months of making puddles, your toddler actually *asks* to pee in the middle of a busy supermarket, and then manages to wait until you can stow the trolley in a corner, nip outside, and then slide his knickers down and plonk the potty beneath him *just* in time. That's achievement!

Although you may have the most boring, worst paid job in the country, it is wise to pause before chucking it in these days. With employment remaining catastrophically high, it could be extremely difficult to find another job should you find that: (1) full-time motherhood is not quite what it was cracked up to be; (2) life on a reduced income is too unpleasant and causing a strain in your marriage; (3) your husband becomes redundant and your job might be the family's salvation; (4) your marriage breaks down and you are left on your own with the children.

Guilt and the Working Mother

First of all, let's talk a bit about guilt, because invariably whenever the subject of working mothers comes up, even these days when it is accepted by psychologists that babies do not suffer from mother deprivation if they have a warm and loving substitute, women still feel guilty. They are further made to feel guilty by some stay-at-home mums who stalk around pronouncing judgement against any woman who sets foot outside her door for useful gain or otherwise.

If the family needs additional income to survive, no one condemns the mother for going out to work. But there is no reason why it should be different if a woman needs to go out to work for her own benefit (or survival?): to continue her job in a field for which she may have trained for years; to continue her job, even an unskilled job that she simply enjoys; to continue her job that she may not particularly like, but that gives her some time in the adult world away from baby-nurturing; to continue her job that supplements the family income.

It's time that women ceased to have to justify wanting to have children *and* a job, if they want to. Men don't have to, so why should women be deprived of doing both? It doesn't mean that a woman loves her children any less. Remember, having a job is not opting *out* of motherhood. In our world as it stands, it is usually taking on the additional role of worker along with that of mother, domestic organizer (housewife), and wife. The difficulty is that you have to make the decision beforehand. No one knows quite how she will react to motherhood until it is heaped upon her.

Maternity Leave

Fortunately, the Maternity Leave laws help a bit. A woman's job must be kept open for her for up to twenty-nine weeks after the baby is born, unless she resigns. But say, after only sixteen weeks, if your baby had dropped the night feeds and settled into some semblance of a routine, there's a bit of a lull (with luck) from the end of the night feeds to crawling which could easily soothe you into thinking that you've made a smooth adjustment and that it wouldn't be too bad to be going on with. After all, it's jolly pleasant to be released from working hours.

Then the baby starts crawling and you're on every-instant-watch to keep him from eating the coal, sticking a paperclip into a socket, or later from lamming a spare brother or sister with a poker. That period from nine to ten months to about twenty months can drive a sane woman to hysteria.

The next phase is what I call 'the falling about time', when stairs have to be climbed and tumbled down, ride-and-scoot toys have to be toppled off, and running and falling is always better than walking and getting there.

But the worst is yet to come and lasts the longest — when they start to talk and ask questions and more questions. It can very quickly cease to be cute or amusing and rapidly become irksome, maddening and excruciatingly frustrating when an insistent little voice keeps asking the same thick-headed, nonsensical question over and over again, no matter how satisfactorily you answer it, and will not leave you a moment's peace even to make a grocery list or to listen to the one o'clock news. This mental torture goes on all day long from the time they can string two words together — 'Wha's 'at?' — until nearly the time when they go to school.

There's a strong case for motherhood in small doses. It's only recently that what sociologists call the nuclear family — that's you, your partner and children — have been separated from the larger, extended family in which the mothering was spread between numerous aunts and grannies and the occasional uncle or grandpa. Even the most devoted mum needs a break now and again, just to regain her adult sanity.

All I am saying is that at the 29-week deadline, when you have to make the decision to go back to your job or not, you are hardly in a position to know what the future holds in order to make an appropriate decision. By the time you are, your job has been filled and it's too late unless you look for another one. If you manage to find one, you will then have a bigger adjustment, taking on a new job rather than just returning to a comfortable old one — and the baby will by then have got used to having you around and kick up more of a rumpus than if you had gone back to work early on.

To Work or Not

The advantages of going back to a full-time job are that:

1) you keep your place in the careers and promotions queue;
2) you may feel the financial draught less with two pay packets;
3) you may continue to feel some sense of achievement;
4) you retain some financial independence;
5) having only limited, precious hours with your offspring, you will probably cherish that time more and *may* use it more positively than if you stayed at home;
6) you retain the mental stimulation (that so many stay-at-home mums miss) of an adult atmosphere.

Some of the disadvantages are that:

1) you become a four-headed gorgon — worker, mother, household organizer, and wife;
2) you are frantically busy and usually exhausted by trying to fulfil all these roles (though mothers who stay at home have similar problems, minus one role);
3) you will doubtless be criticized by someone, be it your mother-in-law, your child's teacher, a friend or foe;
4) you may not actually make much profit after paying tax, stamps, and the nanny or child-minder (or the crêche or day nursery if you're lucky enough to have one near), during the pre-school years, and possibly someone to clean the house;
5) you may worry that your child is not being looked after as you would like;
6) there is always the problem of what to do when the child is ill (rendering you a less dependable employee).

Depending upon your circumstances, a part-time job may satisfy many of your needs. You would not be quite so pressed on the home front, and you would still have half of every day or certain days of the week with your child(ren).

The disadvantages of working part-time are that it may be difficult to find a stimulating or satisfying part-time job, and part-time jobs often pay disproportionately lower than half a full-time job, making it more difficult to show a 'profit' after the child-minder is paid. Also, as a part-time worker, you would probably have to forego promotions until you are once more among the full-timers.

Not to unbalance the odds for returning to some sort of job, let's look at the advantages of staying at home as a full-time mum:

1) you are relatively free after the first few months to fit in various activities around the baby's feeds and naps;

2) you do not have to share the closeness of the one-to-one mother-and-child relationship with a substitute mother figure — your influence is supreme;

3) You have more time to be a wife, mother and housekeeper — whether that means cooking a gourmet meal just occasionally or picking strawberries to make jam. Working mothers have so little time that they must discipline themselves fairly rigidly just to keep up with the absolutely essential domestic chores.

We've already discussed the disadvantages of staying at home and these will become more apparent as the chapters unroll.

The Role of Your Partner

What we haven't touched upon is how much this decision will depend upon your husband's attitudes and willingness to share the burdens. It's no good thinking that you can keep going all hours of the day and night and still come up number one in the cheerful, nice-person-to-live-with stakes. There are only so many hours to the day and so much energy to be spread over all the tasks that you want to cover. When you add another one, something has to give. Either this means that you get cross and unpleasant, if you are unable to keep up to your standards, *or* someone else has to help — husband, cleaner, child-minder, or all of them.

Obviously, if you go back to work, you will need someone to look after your child. If you like your house looking tidy and clean, even if you lower your standards somewhat with young children underfoot, you probably will find that you have to hire someone to come in and clean it at least half a day each week. The alternative is that you, and/or your husband will have to spend half a day doing it at the weekend, or at the end of a very long day.

Cooking, of necessity, will have to be pared down to quickly-prepared meals. You simply won't have the time to get ready for work in the morning, get your child or children up and fed and dressed and, possibly, delivered to a child-minder — and chop up a few vegetables for a casserole. It is likely that you will be much too tired after the dishes are washed and the baby in bed at night to do it then, either, except for the rare occasion. Remember, there is still nappy washing, your own and your husband's clothes to wash and iron, the eternal meal planning and shopping, mending, and later on, toy repairs, and do you have a garden?

Is there *any* leisure time while the children are small, even without a job? My answer is *no*, not unless you have help, and hiring help decreases the money you clear after deductions and the child-minder, especially with a part-time job. It's very easy, if you're not careful, to end up paying for the privilege of going out to work, although I know more than one mother whose retort to that would be: 'What price sanity?'

Whatever you decide simply must be a joint decision between you and your husband, because he will be affected. He will have to show understanding when you come home as tired as he is, wanting to put your feet up just as much as he does. If he takes the attitude that it is your decision to go back to work, and therefore that *you* must sort it out, you might as well give up. You will need his support and encouragement, because you simply can't eliminate eight hours, or even four hours, from every day on the home front and somehow expect, miraculously, that you'll be able to accomplish all that needs doing with the time remaining. He will have to help.

You might divide up the morning tasks: you get the baby up and dressed and fed; he makes the beds, throws the dirty nappies into the washing machine, and gets the breakfast for the two of you, or vice versa. He might do part of the shopping. Or if he's sufficiently adept or willing to be coached, he could prepare or start the preparation of the evening meal every other night, while you give the baby his bath and tuck him in, trading off so that dad gets some of the fun time bathing the baby. I have a friend whose husband does the ironing. He does it better than she does and doesn't mind doing it. She does the gardening and looks after the family's bookkeeping. The point is that no one partner should have to carry an unequal burden. So if you go out to work, the domestic tasks need to be redistributed to even out the work loads — and they will inevitably be greater for both of you.

Waiting Before Returning to Work

From what I've said up to now, you might think that it is wiser to wait until the youngest child goes to school before returning to a job. But there are certain problems which you may not anticipate.

Depending upon your field, in such a fast changing world, technologically, after a break of five to seven years or more, you may find that you have lost track of developments, making it exceedingly difficult to slot back in without retraining. Doubtless, as you won't have been doing the job for whatever length of time, your confidence will be a little shaky. I fear that a good many very capable women never quite manage to pull themselves together for that first interview because they feel that they've somehow fallen behind, and that they are a bit older than the ages specified in the situations vacant adverts. More recently, with such high unemployment, there are far more people chasing every job, dramatically lowering the prospects for anyone who has been out of the job scene for a few years and whose references are stale.

However, you can't keep a good woman down. The obstacles to returning to the job market can be overcome. I suspect that it is because so many women feel unable to prove their ability to a prospective employer that many go off on a completely new tangent and start their own small businesses: home-catering, restaurants, dress shops, beauty salons, office services, estate agents, employment agencies, or whatever.

No one can say when is the best time to return to a job, if at all. The earliest that you might reasonably expect to return would be when the baby is about six weeks old and settled onto a formula, or half formula and half breast-feeding as a friend of mine managed to do against all the odds — breast-feeding the baby in the morning before going to work, a couple of bottle feeds during the day, and then two more breast feeds, one in the evening and one during the night.

The next natural break might be at about six months, after which breast-fed babies can begin to drink cow's milk. If you start weaning the baby off the breast at exactly twenty-four weeks old, you will probably have succeeded within the twenty-nine week limit during which your job will be held open. If you wait any longer, you can count on a wrench as you leave the baby wailing in the child-minder's arms, and that's not an image to fortify you to start a working day, or to bolster you in answering any critics about whether or not you're doing the right thing.

If it's any consolation, most of the babies I've known couldn't care less if it was King Kong who changed their nappies up to about the age of eight months, so long as they didn't actually *see* their mothers putting on their coats and walking out the door. It's sometime after that when consciousness seems to dawn, that mummy is leaving them with Someone Else. If you establish a pattern before then, you're away!

3. Financial Changes

The Cost of a Child

Few couples stop to think about how much having a child will cost. It seems almost sacrilege even to consider such a question, when you think of the love and joy that a child brings, it's like asking the cost of life itself.

But children do cost money, and they go on costing lots of money for a very long time — a minimum of sixteen years, or if they go on to a polytechnic, a college of further education or a university, for twenty-one years — much longer if your child or children decide to become doctors, architects or university professors.

Not to consider whether or not you can afford to have a child is less than kind to the child. Love alone can't buy a cot or a highchair. I can't begin to list all of the costs of rearing a child. Obviously, it will vary from couple to couple, depending upon income and standards. But most of us can remember our own parents at one time or another complaining about the sacrifices they have made for us. And sacrifice it is, when you stop to consider how much more money they would have had available to spend on whatever *they* would have liked instead of having to buy a larger house, to heat extra rooms (all day), to buy us food and clothing, to pay our bus fares, to supply us with training shoes and football gear, toys, violin lessons, films, roller skates, records, pocket money . . . the list goes on and on. Multiply that by however many children there were in your family, or that you hope to have, and the totals are daunting.

Which magazine made a study in December 1977 to try to find out how much people actually do spend on their children. They took an average couple, both working, and calculated how much having one child would cost them over the years taking into consideration the loss of the wife's salary until the child started at school, when she returned to work, thereby boosting the family's total income. Between December 1977 when the study was done and the end of November 1985, the retail prices index rose from 188.4 to 378.4. Adjusting the figures as we go, hold onto your brolly . . .

Which calculated that bringing up one child to the age of 17 would cost the average couple £15,400 (£30,931 in 1985)! This did not take into consideration the cost of hiring a child-minder for £25-35 a week, a nanny at £70 a week, or a private nursery school at £30-50 a week (1985 figures).

You'd like to have two children? The second child, you suggest, will be able to use much of the equipment, toys and clothes that the first has finished using. — *Which* went on to calculate the cost of the same family having a second child, or rather the cost of raising the two children, two years apart, with the wife returning to work when the second reached school age, and the total for the two came to £23,800 in 1977, £47,802 in 1985!

In calculating these figures, *Which* examined how much parents actually spent on their children at different ages (on average) from new born babies through to the age of seventeen. As you might imagine, the older the children became, the more their parents spent on them. If we assume that everything a child needs will have risen in price in proportion to the rise in the retail prices index, the percentage of each pound spent on a child in 1986 would not be much changed.

On the first child *Which* found that parents spent as little as 8p out of every £1 spent, on the baby during the first year. On children from two to four years old, the amount nearly doubled to 15p out of every £1 spent. (Don't forget the slide, the climbing frame, the tricycle and the car-seat.) On children from five to ten, the average family allotted 18p out of every £1 spent on the child. From eleven to fifteen years old, the average went up to 21p out of every £1, rising to 26p out of every £1 spent on children of 16 and 17 years old.

With two children, the average amount spent on the children out of every £1 spent was 8p during the second child's first year, rising to 23p when the eldest child was between 2 and 4 years old, to 30p when the eldest child was between 5 and 10, to 34p when the eldest was between eleven and fifteen, and finally, rising to 39p when the eldest reached the ages of sixteen and seventeen! Nearly 40 per cent of the families' disposable income was spent on the children!

Which didn't go into the cost of private education. Of course, there is a wide variety of fees in private education, depending upon whether you send your child, or children, to a local day school, or whether they become weekly boarders, or full-time boarders. Taking £3,300 as an average for fees as a boarder in a prep school, and £4,500 as an average for fees as a boarder at a public school in 1986, allowing for an annual inflation of 6 per cent from now until your child reaches prep and public schools and throughout his school years his fees at prep school will start at about £5,260 a year by 1994, and his five years at prep school, allowing for 6 per cent inflation, will cost you roughly £29,637! His fees for the first year at public school would be close to £9,600, and the five years spent there would total something in the region of £54,123!

For some reason, girls' schools tend, generally speaking, to be a little less expensive than boys' schools, quoted above, but only by a few hundred pounds a year. Then there are all of the extras — uniforms, sailing, fencing, music lessons, outings and trips abroad.

There are investment plans through which you can pay in lump sums in advance — or Granny can — and let the profits apply to the fees when the time comes.

One such investment organization, the School Fees Insurance Agency Limited of Maidenhead, using the figures above and building in an annual inflation rate of 6 per cent, calculates that if you were able to put down a capital sum as soon as your baby was born in 1986 (and most of us would have to put away a dollop here and a bit there, which would put the total up, although doing it all at once, the sooner the better, would cost you less as the money would have longer to accumulate interest) it would cost you a minimum of £11,142 for the prep school fees, and £12,827 for the public school fees (or £7,857 and £7,273 respectively if a slightly more speculative arrangement were to be made).

Forgetting private education, you might argue that you don't have to pay out the cost of having a child all at once, that you wouldn't really feel it in the dribs and drabs as the years go by. But just divide that total of £30,931 (excluding any school fees) by seventeen years and you come out with just under £2,000 a year. Well, think what *you* could do with another £2,000 a year: a pleasant holiday in the West Indies for the two of you, maybe a new car a year sooner than otherwise; a nicer home if you could pay a slightly higher mortgage; quite a few weekends away; a small boat perhaps; or quite a few gourmet dinners out. I leave you to your own imagination. Remember also that you would have a higher total income — two salaries instead of one.

Even babies cost more than you might imagine. Don't think that three can eat as cheaply as two, or that tiny babies don't eat much. At first, yes, while you are breast-feeding, but they soon get to solid food at about 4 months old. Feeding a baby does cost money, even if you are a dedicated mother who purées yesterday's casseroles and vegetables in the blender. (If you are lucky, your baby may eat it. Mine wouldn't despite my good intentions.) From the baby food stage, the cost of feeding them goes up and up. I have a friend who swears that her eight and nine-year-olds eat as much as she and her husband! The child benefit doesn't go very far when you consider all of the other things you need besides baby food, even at the early stages.

For a start, a couple will probably need a larger house or flat. If you and your husband are living in a one-bedroomed accommodation, if I may digress from finance for a moment, take this advice. Either make a move to a two-bedroomed flat or house *before* the baby is born, or decide to move out of the bedroom when the baby comes home, leave it to the baby, and you and your husband settle down on a sofabed in the sitting-room.

Many couples start out with starry-eyed ideas of togetherness with their new babies in their own room: mum doesn't have so far to go for the night feeds and she can bundle the baby into bed for the feed so that both are cozy and warm. But I can assure you that nothing can put a man, or a woman for that matter, off a baby quicker than being woken up for every wheeze and hiccup, never mind the crying, of a new baby in the same room at night; and newborn babies do make an alarming amount of sniffly, wheezing noises.

So if at all possible, it is a good plan for the baby to have a room of his own and for you to make the move to a new house or flat before becoming so bulbous that you can't help with the packing and unpacking. Trying to arrange things in a new home when you are heavily pregnant is tiring, and if you are tempted to lift anything too heavy it can be dangerous for the baby. Besides, you deserve the peace of mind of knowing that you are ready and settled before the baby's arrival.

Baby Needs

What is necessary in the way of baby clothes and equipment varies with every book you read, most of them erring on the side of way too much. With very careful study of the various lists, a lot of comparative shopping, and talking to other mothers, I pruned the list down to what I considered to be absolutely essential, and bought much of the equipment second-hand. Were I buying it all new in 1986, the total would have come to over £450. It makes the maternity allowance look a bit pathetic!

For your curiosity more than enlightenment, I list here those items that I found to be absolute necessities:

First six to eight months — until the baby sits up

Equipment
Carrycot and wheels
Carrycot mattress
6 carrycot sheets
3 carrycot blankets
Plastic bath
Changing pad
2 nappy buckets (with lids)
Nappy soaking solution
Zinc & Castor oil cream (for
    bottoms)
Baby powder
Cotton balls or small sponge
    (for wiping bottoms)
Baby soap or bath liquid

Clothes
30 nappies (or disposables)
24 Washable nappy liners
8 pairs of rubber pants (or
    waterproof nylon, they last
    longer), not necessary with
    disposables
4 vests
4 terry cloth stretch suits
2 sweaters
2 hats
2 pairs of bootees in winter
Pram suit (or downy zip-front
    sleep suit works as well)

Total: £162 new in 1986.

Optionals
Baby alarm
Pram mobile
Chest of drawers for clothes, bedding, toys, changing on top
Playpen (See Chapter 12)

Total: £69 in 1986.

Six to eight months onwards — sitting, crawling to walking

Cot
Cot mattress

2 sweaters
3 baby coveralls for crawlers

3 fitted cot sheets
3 loose upper sheets
3 blankets
Lightweight pushchair
High chair
Cozy toes for pushchair (if suit has no feet in winter)
2 next-sized terry stretch suits (for sleeping)

4 vests
5 pairs of tights for winter, or socks for summer
1 pair of shoes
Bigger zip-front sleep suit, baby parka, or all-in-one suit for going out

Total: £222 in 1986.

Walking babies

The next sizes of clothes above, plus baby wellies, which are invaluable for preventing wet feet as sodden shoes take a long time to dry, and toddlers love them!

The sum of £453, remember was only for the first lot, through the first six to eight months, and depending upon how quickly your baby grows, you may go through two sizes of terry cloth stretch suits instead of one within that time. If you find these totals daunting, consider that these items were on my list of absolute *minimum* essentials. *Parents* magazine (November 1985) put the cost of having a first baby during the first year at £1,930 — not including washing machine, tumbledrier and second-hand car.

Maternity clothes

During pregnancy, you will need an absolute minimum of a couple of maternity dresses or a pair of trousers and two or three tops (not included in the totals above). If you are watching pennies, my suggestion is to borrow, or buy second-hand, maternity clothes or any of the things for the baby during the first year, especially equipment. You will also need a couple of supportive bras and at least a couple of pairs of maternity knickers, which expand, and later, possibly, breast-feeding bras.

Don't think that you will necessarily go on wearing your maternity clothes after the baby is born. The last thing I wanted to wear once the baby appeared were those maternity clothes that I'd been dying to get out of for the last five months.

Tiny babies couldn't care less whether they have new and expensive clothes, as long as they are warm, dry and comfortable. Nor is there much point until the baby is walking, I maintain, in lavishing what I call 'show-off' clothes on him. He won't take any notice or enjoy them until then, so there is no need for the expense when you are going to cover your baby up under pram blankets, heavy coats or suits to go out in the winter, and nobody can see what he is wearing anyway. It's a bit better in summer, but he will still need a sweater and a pram blanket, at least. Of course, grandparents always like to see their grandchildren dressed up for special occasions, or to be photographed. Knowing this, I dutifully went out and bought each of them a dear little outfit, and they only wore them for the photographs and once or twice afterwards before they had grown out of them.

Babysitting
Once the baby is weaned, or before, if you aren't blessed with a willing, captive granny, friend or sister, there comes the cost of babysitting. If you are really short on cash, a baby-sitting circle is an alternative. They work like co-operatives: you sit for someone else, notching up points for every hour that you sit, usually double points after midnight, and then you 'pay' another mother with your accumulated points. For a breast-feeding mother, this is fairly heavy going for the first few months. She will probably still be tired from interrupted nights, and she must lug (or have help to lug) the carrycot and baby with her wherever she goes to babysit, so that she can feed the baby whenever he is hungry. Her husband *could* take her place as the babysitter, although amongst my acquaintances there are not many husbands who are willing, or sufficiently confident as first-time fathers to know what to do if someone else's baby or toddler wakes up. But despite the effort involved, joining a baby-sitting circle is better than not going out at all, and there is the added bonus that you meet other mothers in the neighbourhood and make friends so that you and the baby can drop in on your walks for a coffee during the day.

Getting back to finance, to give you some idea of how it feels to have the added cost of rearing a child, let's look at a couple with one toddler. To go for an outing, they will need to pay bus fares for two adults and one child. Once at their destination, say the zoo — which as adults they probably wouldn't visit anyway, if it weren't for the child — there are again tickets for two adults and one child. Then there's the bus trip home again.

Add a second child, a pushchair-aged toddler and a four-year-old, and the cost escalates. The zoo tickets alone, excluding the youngest child, who was admitted free, recently cost us £6! And of course, they wanted ice cream cones!

Suppose the family has a car. First the car needs to be equipped with two child-seats in the back seat (end of sports car era for the couple when their children arrive), with each child-seat at a cost of over £30 before dad pulls into the petrol station.

Suppose you decide to go to a pub for lunch with your two offspring, on a fine sunny day. If the pub doesn't serve child portions, you might buy one portion to split between the children — up goes the cost from two to three lunches. Even if you are fortunate to have a pub that does buffet-style lunches, you can at least add 30 per cent more to your bill, and probably more, if you have a finicky eater who decides that he doesn't want pâté, or cheese, or whatever, once he's got it and fancies whatever the kid at the next table happens to have!

Holidays

Once a baby is out of the carrycot, holidays are another crunch. No wonder so many couples with young children opt for a self-catering cottage, caravan or camping. You might well ask yourself, do I really want to move my housekeeping and baby-minding chores to a different, possibly less convenient and more hazardous environment? Yes, a change *is* better than no change, hang the rest!

Should you be among the brave minority — we did it with one, but I lack the moral fibre to try it with two toddlers, one of whom is a bouncing baby boy — who leap to the 'free children under two' offers in the travel brochures, almost always the small print reveals that the free offers don't apply in high season. More often than not, the 'free child' offers melt away into a 50 per cent discount at best, more usually 20 per cent or 10 per cent, and then only if the child or children share the parents' room. If the child(ren) have their own room, you pay for it. And often tour operators cannot even guarantee that the rooms will be adjoining. So, taking a holiday abroad in season can very nearly treble or quadruple the cost of one person going. If you do brave it, there's nothing wrong with May, June or September in Spain, Portugal or Majorca, so go during the low season while you can — before the eldest child starts at school, limiting your holidays to the high season periods.

Ideally, you might have an able-bodied granny or a sister willing to take your offspring off your hands for a couple of weeks so that you and your husband can have a real holiday (less expensive than taking them); or you might hire someone locally to look after them. Otherwise, there are several agencies in London that can provide short-term nannies or granny-type child-minders to look after your children in your own home. This does put up the cost of your holiday, but it might cost less than taking an extra adult along. Of course, you might find yourself worrying about how things were going at home while you are away, but it is a way of getting away.

So it is wise for a couple to take a long, unemotional look at the cost of bringing up and providing for children in the manner they wish. Large families are not necessarily happy families if there isn't enough money to go around. Responsible prospective parents should have a very hard-headed discussion about their financial future and make a realistic assessment of their potential earnings to determine if they can really afford to have a child and continue to live as they would like, or how many children they can afford.

The government does help out if your husband suddenly becomes redundant, of course, or if his earnings are so low that you qualify for supplementary benefit. But ask anyone with a family, even a couple with only one child to support, who is living on the dole and supplementary benefit, and they will tell you that they are existing at a miserable subsistence level. It is better than starving, and no one is condemning the unfortunate people, who through no fault of their own in these days of high unemployment find themselves in this position. But given the choice, surely no one would want to bring a child into such impoverished circumstances.

If the dole is staring you in the face, it is far better to wait to start a family until the tide turns and you can afford to have a child. It is neither fair to you, nor to your child, to put yourself through what is usually a very trying, as well as a physically and emotionally tiring and demanding time, with the additional strain of a child you cannot afford to care for as you wish.

Wait a bit so that the arrival of your child can be a joy — and not a financial burden.

4. Single Parenthood

Only a woman can decide herself whether or not she wants to bring up a baby without the support of a partner, i.e. as a single-parent family. For one thing, a woman may not have a choice. But it may help anyone who finds herself in this position to be a little bit better-prepared if some of the special difficulties are known in advance.

The biggest problem is money. Unless a woman is so lucky as to have inherited a small fortune, or unless she is extremely well paid and can afford not only to keep herself and to hire someone to look after her child while she is working without feeling too great a financial strain, the problem at the root of many of her other problems as a single parent is money.

All the love in the world won't buy that next pair of baby shoes or pay the electricity bill. The hard facts are that babies cost progressively more and more money to provide for, and it takes a lot of money to have them looked after, if the mother doesn't do it herself. If she does look after the child herself it is diabolically difficult to find enough hours in the day, or night, to find some way of earning enough money at home, after the baby has gone to sleep, to make a decent living.

The result is that most mothers in this position, despite their often different and better intentions, have to resort to the maze of benefits offered by the Social Services, which include supplementary benefit, child benefit, single parent supplement, rates rebates and rent support. To a seventeen-year-old who has never held a job, and never supported herself, juggling a budget for the first time to cover rent, food, electricity and gas, clothes, transport and entertainment, the amounts available through the various benefits may sound like a lot. In truth, even the maximum for which any mother (or father) might qualify will leave her and her child at the very lowest level of subsistence.

A girl may face the situation with stoicism and great strength of character while her baby is small, thrilled with her new baby and happy to sacrifice her own needs for those of her child. But as soon as the child starts at playgroup or school, she will inevitably feel her own child making comparisons with how many toys other children have, the outings that other children's parents can afford to take them on, the holidays that other children enjoy. Apart from the self-sacrifice necessary, and it is enormous, this feeling that she is not able to give her child as many toys or treats as other two-parented children have, hurts, and it hurts a great deal.

Other children can be terribly cruel and incredibly boastful, mercenary little wheeler-dealers: 'My mum has a new BMW, what kind of a car does *your* mum have?' 'Look, I got a watch for *my* birthday. What did *you* get for yours?' '*We* live in a house with four bedrooms. How many bedrooms do *you* have?' 'How much pocket money do *you* get?' 'What did *you* get for Christmas?' Also, while we're on the subject of other children's cruelty, in spite of there being one single-parent family out of every eight in the U.K., there is almost invariably the kid who will ask: 'Does your dad make a lot of money?' 'What does your dad do?' 'Well, where *is* your dad?' 'Don't you even *know* him?'

This lack of money means lack of freedom — and leisure — for the mother. She will probably not be able to afford a car. Even frequent bus journeys are out of the question. Counting every penny means that she won't have the money to go out herself very often, won't be able to buy nice clothes to wear when she does, and paying a babysitter, if there is no one she can beg to sit free, adds to the cost of going out. The result: no social life for the mother!

One single mother I know manages to get a neighbour to babysit for her for one hour, one evening every week, so that she can go out and play badminton. But not to take undue advantage of her kind neighbour, she feels that she must rush straight back, and the only social life she has, really, is if she invites someone back to her house for coffee.

Another mother goes to the Pre-School Playgroup evening course to learn how to assist at a playgroup when her child is old enough, thereby at least meeting other mothers. But what a far cry from her single days when she was free to go out whenever and with whomever she liked, to meet new people, to enjoy new activities on the spur of the moment.

This constant lack of money means that unless a mother has a generous volunteer to babysit free for her, or unless she is lucky enough to join a babysitting rota and can babysit for someone during the day so that she can bring her own child along (her own child's need to sleep renders her unavailable to babysit at night), she will have virtually no social life of her own after the baby's bedtime — and none in the daytime unless she brings her child along.

The tie of looking after her child leads inevitably to loneliness. Like any other new parent with a child or two to fit her activities around, she will tend to lose contact with her old, single friends. Further, without the ready money for a babysitter — to buy her freedom — she is literally tied to her home in the evenings while her child sleeps.

Even worse than not having a social life, and that's hard enough for any young woman who may see the years stretching out before her without even the prospect of an opportunity to find romance, if ordinary mothers of two-parent families feel starved of adult conversation, multiply the single mother's need a hundred-fold. With no one to come home at night to talk over the day's experiences, she is caught in an emotional straight-jacket without a release button. Add sexual frustration to this general frustration, and viewed from a vantage point over years, until she is able once again to establish some sort of social life, the prospect looks bleak indeed.

The single mother may make daytime friends with other mothers who have husbands. But the social lives of couples with children, if they have any, tend to revolve around other couples. Looking at my own life, this isn't meant to be stand-offish. It's simply a question of logistics: fit two average-sized adults and two child seats, or worse, one child seat and one carrycot, into a normal-sized car and there is no room for anyone else. So if we should want to invite even one person who doesn't have a car to go somewhere with us, we have to take two cars, which doubles the petrol and rather spoils things as a family outing.

Gingerbread, the organization for single parents, makes a brave effort to try to overcome some of the problems of single parenthood by organizing social gatherings for parents, outings for their children, and cheap holidays.

But whatever way you look at it, parenthood is a difficult and demanding job. Single parenthood is *more* than doubly so.

5. Baby-Bashing —
Am I the Sort Who Might?

Not me, you shriek! But please believe me, everyone, every parent at one time or another is tempted. Don't think that you will be immune. No matter how much you may want him or how much you love your baby, you won't be able to help feeling very angry occasionally in the face of how totally irrational, unreasonable, frustrating and provoking a small child can be.

Take a newborn baby who won't stop crying in the middle of the night. Tired as you are, you may take the sensible approach that the baby wouldn't cry unless there was something wrong, that he needed something — to be fed, changed, tucked in again, another blanket — or he wouldn't cry. You may become alarmed that the baby is suffering some pain that he can't tell you about. Naturally, you will try virtually everything that you can think of to soothe and pacify him. But finally, when you have done all this, when you have gone back to bed and lie there desperately trying to get back to sleep, and the baby starts to cry yet again . . . you might well be tempted when you get up, once again, to go into the baby's room and give him a good shake or a thump. Anything to make him stop! But *don't* — shaking can cause irrevocable brain damage.

It once happened to me, one morning when my baby girl was about six months old; she refused to suckle, turning her little face away, crying pitifully. I tried everything, changed her nappy, changed her clothes and bedclothes. No amount of cuddling, cooing, or gripe mixture (for colic) had any effect. The crying went on and on, searing my very soul. In my arms, she was a small squirming, kicking, arch-backed fury. I grew frightened, desperate, frustrated, and finally, angry. How dare she reject all of my efforts, how dare she when I was trying my very best?

I caught myself wanting to shake her, wanting to thump her, *anything* to arrest her attention, to shock her into silence. Suddenly, I realized how and why people batter tiny babies. The more one cares, I suspect, the more desperate one can become, wanting to stop the crying. It isn't so much the annoyance of the noise, it is the deep frustration, the exasperation and sense of total failure at not being able to relieve whatever is causing the baby's anguish.

In the end, after ringing the health visitor for advice, I gritted my teeth and put her down to cry herself to sleep behind a closed door. In the afternoon, she took a little milk, and in the evening, she went off to sleep earlier than usual, presumably exhausted from the crying. Next day, she seemed back to normal.

Or take an older child, a toddler at the stage when he has begun to understand 'yes' and 'no', who insists on banging his sister or brother over the head, or pulling hair in order to snatch a coveted toy away from the other. You may stand there saying, 'Don't pull Timothy's hair', until you are blue in the face, and the naughty toddler will go right on as though you were a thousand miles away. The temptation to belt him is great!

Or suppose you have a toddler who throws temper tantrums whenever you try to get him off the swings at the playground to come home to tea. There you are, your toddler screeching at the top of his lungs, attracting the attention of all of the other mums and children in the playground, and you trying to collar him into his pushchair as he flings his arms and legs in all directions, finally resorting to a sit-down howling strike. Don't tell me you wouldn't be tempted.

Or suppose you run through an obstinate streak when your toddler utterly refuses to comply with any simple request you might make. Oh yes, we are all tempted.

The healthy response is not to feel guilty about getting that angry at your child. After all, it's only natural. Most of baby books tell you not to try to hide your anger from your child — he has to learn about anger sometime. There comes a time when every child, it seems, goes through a period of trying you to see just how far he can push you and what happens then . . .

The trick is neither to let the child win, nor to lose your temper and control completely — and not to feel too guilty if you end up screaming! To triumph in these circumstances is extraordinarily difficult and demands not only the determined self-control of a saint, but the subtlety of a diplomat, not to mention the ingenuity of an inventor. When pushed to extremity, I have found that the best immediate action is to put distance between me and the child. This gives both of us a chance to simmer down, and the moment to pass.

Let's look at what you might have done in the above situations.

With the newborn baby, once you are satisfied that there is nothing medically wrong (which isn't easy for an inexperienced mother with her first baby), the best solution is to put as many thick doors between you and the baby as you can manage, even if that means curling up in an armchair in the sitting room for a quarter of an hour. Then you *might* be ready to go in again, to pick up the baby to give him another rock, to sing him yet another lullabye, or to play him some music on the record player. Sometimes a ride in the car will send a howling baby off to sleep; even if it means dressing in the middle of the night, sometimes desperate measures are necessary.

With the toddler who bashes or pulls his brother's or sister's hair, one solution I've found, once you've extricated the victim, is to smack the offender's hand until he takes notice and then to put him behind a thick door, without the toy, for five minutes. Of course, he'll cry. But you won't have bashed him and by the time he comes out, he can be comforted and told that we don't go around bashing people or pulling hair.

I know some mothers who think the best policy is to let kids sort it out, i.e. wait until the child who is being attacked retaliates. That's one solution in an aggressive world, but I prefer to try to teach them to be civilized, at least to each other.

There really is no easy answer to a temper tantrum, especially one staged in public. Some mothers bribe with sweets. But why reward the crime? My inclination is simply to sweep the little fury into the air and if he's not flailing around too dangerously, to whirl him around fast. In his surprise at being suddenly whipped up, he might, just might, stop screeching and be sufficiently distracted by the movement to accept it as a game as you swing him down and into the pushchair.

The obstinate streak is more difficult to deal with because the temptation is to try to out-last the child in your own obstinacy. You might try challenging the child: 'I'll bet you can't . . .' whatever it is you want him to do; but he's apt to see through it. With obstinacy there is not much point in trying to out-last the obstinate streak, so try total distraction. Change the child's focus of attention to another irresistible subject before returning to your request. With a bit of luck, the time lag might have taken the heat out of his anger so that he can respond without being seen to lose face. Some very young children are as full of pride and as stubborn as adults. Somehow you have to stop banging the stone wall of his will and find a way round instead. It is not easy when you are furious yourself!

If *nothing gives,* you must retaliate somehow without belting him. Otherwise, his obstinancy will have won and he will try it again and again.

Dealing with Tension

If none of the situations above seems to you the sort that would push you to the point of hitting a child (and by this I don't mean smacking the bottom or a slap on the hands), try to imagine them in the context of one of those days when everything goes wrong, as many days do when you are mothering small children, when you are at the end of your tether and one more thing is just too much. Tension accumulates, and the only relief, other than the transquillizers which many doctors prescribe for mothers of young children, is to get away. A mother should; she must; she owes it to herself, and her child. She will be a better mother, when she feels the pressure rising, if she removes herself from the cause of the pressure.

It sounds simple, put like that, and very obvious. But it isn't always easy for a mother to find someone who will trade off babysitting with her so that each of them can have a morning or an afternoon off. Often a woman may feel, and correctly so, that she is at such a low ebb that the last thing she could possibly take on is someone else's child as well.

If money is too short to hire a babysitter, and it often is, one solution is that used by a friend of mine, who takes her children out, somewhere, every afternoon just so that when they all begin to get tired and their nerves frayed, they are either out in the open air or distracted by other people. When the weather is fine, she takes them for long walks, to the park, or dawdles through the shops. When it rains, she tries to visit a friend with children or invites someone with children to visit her. *Sharing* even the most maddening situations can turn them into a laugh. Having a time limit to the torture also helps her to keep a stiff upper lip — 'As soon as we have lunch, we'll go out for a walk'.

Another solution is to grumble to friends. Commiserating about how fractious the children are can take the steam out of the situation. Telling it often brings out the humour of the tale. If you feel that you couldn't bare your soul to a friend, or haven't one who has suffered through young children, there are always the Samaritans at the end of a telephone; and in some towns there is a kind of Parents Anonymous number, usually answered by other mothers who have been through the same trying times. It is a widespread and well recognized problem.

For advice about how to handle any problem that might relate to health, you can contact your health visitor, a social worker, and certainly, your doctor.

Apart from physical violence, a recent American study has analysed other ways that parents may damage their children: 1) physical or emotional neglect; 2) emotional abuse; 3) sexual exploitation. The study revealed that physical violence most often occurs when a parent has a background of emotional or physical deprivation, and was often abused, himself or herself, as a child. Emotional neglect or abuse occurs when the child is seen by the parent as unlovable or disappointing. Any of these abuses might be triggered off by a crisis, or when a parent has no effective lifeline — no one to turn to, or no way to get away.

As analysed in this study, child batterers and abusers of children most often fell into one of these categories: sociopaths; sadists (those who enjoy inflicting pain or suffering on others); fanatics of one sort or another; parents addicted to drink or drugs; either very young and therefore immature parents, or parents who were mentally retarded or having a low IQ. In short, they were people who were lacking the mental or emotional stamina to deal with the situation as a mature adult.

It may be blatently obvious to say that one mustn't beat a child. We all know this, and may feel that we never would. But the National Society for the Prevention of Cruelty to Children estimates that 7,038 children were physically abused in England and Wales in 1984, based on figures of cases reported to them. These figures do *not* include those cases reported to the Social Services and *not* reported to the NSPCC, and they do not touch the tip of the iceberg of unreported cases.

It is just as well to realize that no matter how appealing and sweet children may look, they can be infuriating little creatures, and too often a parent's natural response when a child refuses to respond in a reasonable way is to react like a child — hitting out. As adults, we must somehow rise above the most dreadful provocations, accepting our own anger as normal, and channel that anger into a form of retaliation that will triumph over the child.

There's a challenge for you as a parent! One of my friends swears by pounding a teddy bear, together with her child, when they get really angry at one another!

6. Babies — How They Differ

Before having a baby, without giving it much thought, I assumed that somehow parents' personalities, and the way in which they treated their babies, pretty much determined how babies respond. A few years and two babies later — and most of the mothers I have talked to agree — I find that a baby's reactions and responses to his parents are only half the picture. Babies come not only in all sizes, shapes and colours, but having a panoramically wide variety of temperaments and needs. What I hadn't realized was how well formed a baby's personality seems to be from the moment of birth.

This is not to say that babies and children don't change as they are moving from one period of development into another, or that the development of their personalities is in any way predictable. Not a bit of it. A real howler of a baby may turn out to be an absolute charmer as a toddler and, in turn, develop into a cheeky mischief maker at his second birthday, easing into a co-operative helper when his first permanent teeth appear, only to shrink into a shy gawky child at puberty, who settles into a reasonably well co-ordinated, well-balanced teenager. And any of a million variations!

There's no telling what kind of a baby you might have, physically, mentally, or emotionally. To be sure, how a child is treated has some effect, I think. But, and it's a big *but,* every baby seems to spring into the world with his own set of emotional and physical responses from the instant of birth.

Don't laugh when I tell you that when I was expecting our first child I listened to a lot of lovely music. Having read that newborn babies seem to enjoy Mozart but not Beethoven, and especially any music with a high melodic line such as flute or violin concertos, I listened to a lot of concertos. If newborn babies respond to good music, I reasoned, who knows what the unborn baby can hear in the womb? It couldn't hurt, I thought, and maybe hearing a lot of lovely music would soothe the baby and make him placid. Who knows? The baby was neither terribly placid nor otherwise. Who knows how she *might* have turned out without the music? Much the same, I suspect.

What has become very obvious is that both our children are very, very different, and have been from birth — and both got the music treatment! The little girl has always been winsome, eager to please, willing to sit on my lap while visiting strangers for hours, gentle, and very observant. The little boy, from day one, has been impatient — to be fed, to move about constantly — full of bluster, brave to the point of foolhardiness, aggressive to get his own way, and a joker. Just the difference between boys and girls, you might say, but that's another subject.

Psychologists are fond of doing studies to show how mothers — it's always mothers — condition their boys and girls, not to mention first, second, and subsequent children, differently. Certainly, it's true. We do tend to put baby girls in small dresses and tell them even in their carrycots how beautiful and sweet they are, and the boys how gorgeous and sweet they are. It's not long before the girls are given dolls and the boys teddy bears, the girls get prams and the boys toy lorries, and the girls learn to help with setting the table, and the boys, too, at least at our house. But it's odd how the girls do seem to gravitate towards dolls, and the boys most decidedly towards anything with wheels! We do, nevertheless, subtly treat the sexes differently, if in nothing else, in the clothes we put on them.

But how we really treat them differently is in *our* responses to *their* behaviour, reinforcing their differences. I don't find my little boy looking after his teddy like my little girl does her dolly; teddies are for him to cuddle, for *his* convenience and comfort. Can it be that we are born with motherly instincts for caring? Or that little girls already at this tender age identify with their mothers? It is dangerous territory for amateur pyschologists to tread.

But to return to the wide variety of babies: you might have a newborn who sleeps and feeds every five, four, three, or two hours, or one who feeds completely irregularly. You might have one who always has wind and can't go back to sleep until he burps, or one who never has wind. You might have one who cries and cries with colic, or one who only seems to cry when he needs something, to be fed, changed, to be made warmer or cooler.

After the first few months, you may find that you have a baby who still likes to sleep, practically around the clock, or one who likes to be awake a lot of the time, propped up in a bouncing chair watching whatever you are doing.

A little later, you might discover that you have a baby who will go easily to strangers or one who howls incessantly until he is back in your arms (start early, getting him used to someone else). You might find that you have a 'clinger', a child who tenaciously hangs onto your skirts or trousers whenever there are strangers around, or one who readily moves away from you to investigate any new surroundings and playmates. Your toddler might willingly share his toys with other children or he might battle to the death over not just a favourite teddy bear, but any toy that another child happens to pick up. You might have a physically adventurous or a cautious child, one who chatters once he gets to the talking stage, or one who doesn't say much. You may have a child who sings, or one who never utters a note without heaps of encouragement from you.

You might have a baby who insists upon eating or trying to eat coal, sand, dirt, or anything that comes to hand, or one who discovers after only one try what is tasty and what is a bit gritty and nasty. Your child might be docile and eager to please, or with a will of his own and a temper to match. They can both be in the same family, I assure you, and I can't believe that the only reason is their difference of sex or order of arrival.

There is just no predicting what kind of a baby you may have, or how he will change through the weeks, months and years. This is not to say that the books advising how to deal with temper tantrums or what are called the 'terrible two's' or other behavioural problems are useless. It *is* possible to mould and shape your child's responses, to a certain extent. But don't think that you can change a child's basic personality.

Let me give you an example. The baby books are almost united in their advice about toddlers who wake up repeatedly in the night. Whatever you do, they say, don't bring the child into your own bed. This, the books warn, serves as a reward for the child's having woken up. But friends who have suffered from this problem not just over a period of weeks or months, but for years, say that tired and exhausted as you become under these circumstances, what else are you to do? After getting up the third or fourth time, cuddling the child, reading a story and hoping the child has fallen asleep, only to have him burst into tears yet again as you try to tiptoe out of the room . . . the only way to keep the peace and get a little sleep is to take the child into your bed.

Sometimes, installing a night light, or not feeding the child cheese for evening tea, may eliminate the problem. Sometimes nothing helps. But leaving the child to cry doesn't change him from being a child who wakes up in the night. He will continue to wake up in the night.

We are lead to believe, until science can prove otherwise, that there are no good and bad babies, only easy and difficult babies. Being good or bad suggests a degree of self-conscious wilfulness which a baby is supposed to be incapable of, at least, so we think. Just when they become capable of conscious decision-making is highly debatable.

The other day a friend laughed heartily when I shrieked at my twenty-one-month-old, that he was naughty because he had upset a cup of coffee quite deliberately. 'He can't possibly know what you're saying,' she said. But he jolly well does know what I'm saying when I ask him to come and get his coat on; he comes. Or if I ask him to go and look for his bottle, he toddles off and comes back with the bottle. And he knows what 'No' means. He will usually stop whatever he's doing to look up and find out why I am saying 'No'.

So why shouldn't he understand when I tell him that upsetting a cup of coffee is naughty, or more precisely, that he is not to do it the next time? To be sure, he had no way of knowing what the result of upsetting the cup would be in advance, he simply did it. But now he knows that mummy didn't like it, *if* he is at a stage when he can remember.

This growing of the toddler's ability to remember what is acceptable and not acceptable behaviour is so subtle while it is happening that it's much easier to know when it has already happened and he remembers 'No' the next time.

My homespun theory, is to speak to the baby as though he understands, and one day he does; rather than waiting until the child seems old enough to understand what is right and wrong. In my humble experience this dawning awareness, the sudden positive response to a mother's request or command, can take place anytime between the baby's first sitting up and just under the age of two. If a mother never makes any requests, how is she to know when the baby understands by responding?

At some point or another, babies do seem to go through a stage of wanting to please, even if they've ignored you totally up until then. The trick is to be ready for it, for from that moment on you can begin to teach the baby what might be harmful to him, and more positively, to show him how to place one block on top of another, how to climb the stairs, how to throw a ball, and to accept you as his guide through a baffling world.

7. Changing Relationships

With Your Husband

> With growing pleasure, my husband and I would stand peering over her carrycot as she discovered how to bang the carrycot rattle to make a noise; we were elated when she began to grasp a ring of rattles, and eventually, when she learned to kick in her bouncing cradle to rock herself.

If your marriage is shaky, have a baby! How many times have you heard that old myth? But nothing — apart from adultery, possibly — could put more strain on a marriage than having a baby! Tear yourself away from the joyful images of beaming new parents and their newborn babies for a moment and take a look at some of the realities.

With the arrival of a new baby, your entire lifestyle must change. From your husband's point of view, suddenly, your attention is no longer focused on him. Your first duty is to look after the baby. This doesn't mean that you have lost interest in him, but it does mean that your attention is divided between him and the baby and, usually, the baby's needs come first, and his come second.

Put like this, it sounds fairly obvious, and nothing that a normal mature male couldn't accept. But just picture your husband's face if he were to walk in after a day's work to have the howling baby thrust into his arms, when all he really wants to do is to go and change his clothes and sit down and put his feet up until supper is ready. With you at the point of tears and the dinner boiling over on the cooker, it's not a soothing scene to come home to; and if in your eagerness to get supper on the table, you ask him to change a smelly nappy and tuck the baby in, unless you have discussed all this beforehand, well . . . I leave you to guess his reaction. Or suppose the howling baby needs to be breast-fed, so you ask your husband to mind the supper while you give the baby a feed. Whatever way you look at it, it's an extension to his working day, just when he thought he'd come to the end of it. While a new mother might well be thinking that her husband is jolly lucky to have only an eight-hour working day, this is not a propitious time to remind him of it!

Nor does your working day end when the baby is tucked up into bed, unfortunately. The supper might be on the table, and your husband just starting to tell you what the boss said, when there is a wail from upstairs.

You try to concentrate, but the wailing continues, and there is nothing for it — you must go up to find out what is the matter, leaving your husband in mid-sentence and your own supper to get cold. It may be no more than a soiled nappy, but that can take a few minutes to change. Nor is leaving the baby to cry a solution: you would gobble your supper too quickly and only half hear what your husband is saying, anyway, trying to get up to tend to the baby.

Let this happen a few times more during the evening, as it often does, and you can easily give up trying to have a reasonable conversation with your husband. By that time you are so tired that you're aching to go to bed — and to sleep. From you husband's point of view, you are no longer quite as available as you were, either to talk to at the end of his day, to go out with (you must look after the baby and any going out has to be 'organized') or even as much of a lover.

Just when greater demands are being put upon your husband — the pressure to keep his job and the necessity of taking on more domestic chores — he feels your sudden lack of support, for the simple reason that you need *his* support. During the first few weeks or months of the baby's life, you will both be operating under conditions of extreme fatigue caused by loss of sleep due to night feeds — unless you happen to be married to one of those sound sleepers who would need a near-exploding bomb to wake him. If you are, that too can cause extra strain and resentment between you. So you are both making monumental adjustments at a time when you are both, through physical exhaustion, considerably under par.

Planning ahead

One of the ways to alleviate some of this strain is to discuss before the baby is born, how you intend to cope. By planning ahead, even a mountain of tiredness can be reduced if not to a mole hill at least into perspective. But it is astonishing how having a baby can broaden the spectrum for disagreement with your nearest and dearest. Questions will arise which, if not thoroughly discussed and resolved before they occur, can create a dreadful see-saw between two partners holding different points of view.

For a start, you might discuss these:

Should you let the baby cry or go to him immediately, no matter what you are doing?

Should the father do one night feed, or perhaps both night feeds, every other night (if you are bottle feeding)? If you are breast-feeding, should he get up with you occasionally? Most men take the attitude that they have to be fresh for their new all-important jobs as there is only one salary to support the family. But a mother is also fully occupied during the day and physically weakened from childbirth with little chance to recoup her strength unless she has the opportunity for unbroken sleep.

How soon should you leave a newborn baby with a babysitter so that the two of you can go out, even briefly, if you are breast-feeding?

Should you feed the baby 'real' food or baby food?

When the baby starts to crawl, and later, to walk, the scope for disagreements and arguments widens even more. Should you put anything and everything dangerous out of sight and reach, or try to 'teach the baby' that some things are not to be touched? Should babies be smacked or merely told 'No-No' until you're hoarse? Should babies be allowed to walk around without wearing shoes even on cold floors in the winter? How soon, if at all, should children be allowed sweets, crisps, biscuits and soft drinks, as opposed to savoury biscuits and natural fruit juices? Should you allow a child to interrupt adult conversations? Should you insist that a child eat all of his food or throw what he doesn't want away? Should you try to teach him to read, or at least to know the alphabet and his numbers, at home or wait until he gets to school? All of these vexed questions will arise and may as well be solved, better now than later in the heat of the moment.

The areas of contention broaden as the days, months and years go by. How should you punish? Should you give 'free' pocket money or expect some duties to be performed to earn it? How much pocket money? What will the child be expected to use it for — sweets only, or coveted records, sporting equipment, outings, movies, presents for others?

Many of the answers to these questions depend upon how we ourselves were brought up, not necessarily because we want to bring up our children in the same way, but often because we do not. All of these questions need to be aired between parents so that they can make joint decisions, even though it may be a compromise between them, in order to present a united front to the children (and the in-laws).

Sex

Besides these areas of disagreement that may suddenly spring up between you and your husband, much more will be happening to your relationship. If one day you suddenly realize that you do not feel quite as close to him as you once did, well, probably you aren't. In Latin America, where men are notoriously unfaithful, there is a saying, 'Fidelity until the first child'. Only now as a mother do I understand what they mean and why. It isn't quite as damning against Latin lovers as I had previously thought. It's simply that, with very few exceptions, mothers of new babies are not very interested in sex, if at all!

What! You may say? Well, let's look at the facts. A new mother is up at least once or twice a night for a minimum of a half hour each time, usually nearly an hour each time; she is exhausted from lack of sleep, even if she does try to catch up by taking cat naps in the morning or afternoon or whenever she can. When she finally gets to bed all she wants is sleep and nothing else!

If the night feeds last for ten days, lucky you. You can begin to recuperate, not just physically, but sexually, if you like. Let the night feeds go on for six, eight or nine months or longer, with the resultant interrupted sleep, and you won't have much energy left for sexual activities. Just lying there can seem an effort, never mind anything more active.

Add to that several facts which never seem to be discussed. If you happen to have an episiotomy and stitches, or tears and stitches, you may be extremely tender and sore in those parts for quite a long time. Spermacidal jelly helps lubrication, but it may be months before you can look forward to insertion without pain or a secret dread of being hurt — even after the most stimulating sex play.

I swear that after my first child I was sewn up much tighter than ever I had been before having the child. It was not unlike being a virgin all over again, with considerable pain, not just the first time but over and over again, and that was not a nice experience. Even though you may know intellectually that it is temporary and that the pain will ease with time and 'exercise', it does not make love-making an experience to look forward to.

Although I hate to sound negative towards breast-feeding — I'm not, I am very strongly in favour as it is the best, safest way to give your baby the right nutrition and protective immunity — while you are breast-feeding, and wearing those drop-front bras and nipple shields to keep from dribbling through your clothes, well, you may feel beautifully maternal, but you don't feel like much of a sex object. Most women have to sleep in the wretched bras or wake up in a wet bed, and the same goes during love-making, unless you line the bed with large bath towels. So much for spontaneity! It is much easier just to drop off to sleep, unless you can view the whole thing as a huge hoot!

Social life

There is another rather nebulous area that is not much discussed. When a couple become a family, with the ties that are involved in looking after a child, their outward activities usually shrink, in favour of more inward-looking activities. Perhaps a wife used to play tennis, go to yoga, and meet some of her single girlfriends occasionally for a night out. Perhaps her husband jogs, plays village cricket or football, and likes to prop up the bar at the pub with his mates occasionally. But when a baby arrives most of these activities, certainly the mother's, will go by the way for a while. In the first instance, it will be while she is recovering from childbirth and during the first few months of breast-feeding and getting up in the night to do the feeds. For a time, she simply won't feel like going out, and it seems churlish to make her husband stay at home just because she's not feeling up to going out. Later on, it's not so easy to pick up her yoga-tennis-girls'-night-out pattern again. She must either make sure that her husband, or a babysitter, can look after the baby.

While a husband is still free to follow his leisure activities, it is easy to see why many new mothers resent their husbands retaining the freedom they have lost. Nights out, either together or separately, have to be carefully co-ordinated and planned. Which activities will the new mother try to keep up and which will she let go?

If I may put in a suggestion, as soon as you feel fit enough, get out! Even a breast-feeding mum can usually get away for an hour or an hour-and-a-half during the evening, unless you are cursed with a baby who sleeps all day and stays awake all evening. If yours sleeps in the evening, plan to go out regularly with your husband, once a week, if possible, to see friends, to pop into a pub, to go to the cinema, or to take an evening class that you are both interested in. This last is a terrific, cheap diversion as you are forced to think about something other than the baby. Also, having paid your money in advance, you will probably make a special effort to attend, not just let your evening out slip by if it's slightly inconvenient.

It takes real determination not to let your life crumple inwards. If you let it, one day you may wake up wondering what it's all about. Mothering is a lot of give, give, give; and unless you organize some little treats for yourself, before you know what's happened, you can find yourself at the bottom, in the depths of depression, wondering how on earth you got there. How you got there is of being constantly at someone else's beck and call, twenty-four hours a day, day in and day out. By trying to retain some tiny piece of your own existence, for some activity that you really enjoy, with your husband preferably, you will be taking steps to avoid ending up feeling like everybody's dishmop, a martyr without a cause.

I remember the reaction of one of my single friends after a weekend's visit early in the breast-feeding, night-feeding era. 'Why, *you* don't have *any* fun! You no more finish feeding the baby than you've got to start making an adult meal. When that's over, it's the dishes, or the nappies, or the baby's awake and crying.'

She was right, and you can get to feeling very sorry for yourself very quickly unless you do something for light relief once in a while. Your feeling worn out and hard-done-by doesn't make you a very pleasant person to live with either, so decide how you are going to alleviate the symptoms before they get to you. It can be done. It's only a matter of choosing and making the effort to follow through. So it may not be the time to study French for the first time, or to leap into a keep-fit class, not until you recover some of your energy, but it may be the time to take up chess, join a local women's group where you can go and listen to interesting talk, or learn a craft. But make a point of getting out, singly if you must, but sometimes with your husband. You owe it to both of you to protect that feeling of twosome, the togetherness that has been shattered by the arrival of the baby, no matter how welcome.

With Relatives

There is nothing, it seems, like getting pregnant for opening the door to advice from all quarters, most especially from your own mother or your mother-in-law. Suddenly, even though up to now they may have clasped their own opinions to their bosoms, you are in a vulnerable position. You are totally inexperienced in the realm of having children, and they, by virtue of having produced at least one, maybe even thirty years ago, are the experts.

Even if previously you got on splendidly with your mother or mother-in-law, having babies in the 1980s is *not* the same as having them all those years ago, and you can count on being told in great detail how it all was way back then. Equipment, toys and baby clothes have improved, and fashions in child-rearing, like fashions in everything else, have changed, too. It's just as well to try to keep that idea of fashion in mind, so that the atmosphere doesn't get too charged over whether to breast or bottle feed; whether the baby should have a bassinet, a Moses basket, or a carrying pouch; whether to buy a new or used pram; whether or not the baby should be left out in the pram on chilly days 'to get some fresh air'; whether you should give the baby commercially-prepared baby food or perhaps your own; how soon the baby should be allowed to eat certain foods; the terrible drama of sweets or no sweets; whether or not you should go back to work and when; how soon you and your husband should go out together leaving the baby — the list is endless and, I suspect, will plague mothers for the rest of their children's growing-up years.

You begin to see, probably, why it is so important for you and your husband to have discussed all this extraordinarily pernickety nitty-gritty before you are assailed in public debating territory unprepared, i.e. without knowing how your beloved feels about the merits of terrycloth nappies versus disposables, or dummies.

It is easy to say, listen to the advice and then make up your own mind, but in all honesty, without previous experience, you have very little basis upon which to make these decisions. Most of us, let me assure you, feel naturally more inclined to listen to the advice of sisters and friends of about the same age, with whom we have more in common. If for no other reason than that they have been through the experience more recently, made the decisions based on more or less what is available currently, and remember it all very clearly, because the experience is so close to them — what was or was not a good choice, and why.

Our mothers, bless them, probably remember their mother-hood through glasses tinted by rosy mists of memory, and therefore, we are right to suspect, sometimes, that they may not recall things exactly as they were. If you have an advice-prone mother or mother-in-law, her answer to this is that babies don't change — it's the same having a baby now as it was in her day. But it isn't.

When some of us were born, it was the usual practice for babies to be born at home. Now they are born in hospitals or maternity homes, unless you strenuously insist against it. There was a period when it was the fashion to bottle feed; now medical research has proved that breast milk is far better suited to a newborn baby than any formula and, in addition, provides extra protection against disease.

When we were born, not many people had washing machines. Now everyone who can possibly afford to buy even an old twintub at a local auction does so. If they can, they buy an automatic to save the transfer from one tub to the other. Now there are liquid bath soaps, which babies prefer, rather than soaping them all over the old-fashioned way before popping them — usually slithering — into the bath. There are nappy soaking solutions, which sterilize the nappies and keep them from smelling between washings, the sprays to keep your nipples from getting tender, and the cream to keep you from getting stretch marks.

So you can only listen attentively and accept whatever portion of the advice seems sound to you, trying to hedge diplomatically as you go. What we as new mothers all too often forget is that our mothers and mothers-in-law are just as thrilled by the anticipated arrival of the new baby as we are, and they want the very best possible and feel some responsibility for their new grandchild.

Having help
This feeling of responsibility often takes the shape of a mother or mother-in-law volunteering to 'help out' for a few days after the new mother comes home with the baby. Unless you have an exemplary, honest-to-the-bone relationship with whichever mother figure has made the offer, you would do far better to decline.

In the first place, you as a new mother will be very tired and, as a result, not up to dealing with strained relations. The kind of help you really need is that of an all-round housekeeper; someone to do the shopping, cook the meals for you and your husband, someone to put the nappies in the washing machine and to hang them out, someone to clean the house and do the ironing — *your husband*, if he can get the time off.

Unless you have a hyper-sympathetic mother or mother-in-law, what she will want to do is to look after the baby, leaving you to do the housework just when what you need to be doing is to develop a warm and close bond with the baby, learning to care for him, and resting to recoup your lost energy. But it isn't easy for a young mother in her own home to sit and watch as her older mother or mother-in-law gets more and more tired as she gets on with the work. The chances are that you would be tempted to help, both of you working away when *you* ought to be resting. But she can rest when she gets home. It might be months before you will have an unbroken night's sleep!

Having a house guest is also a strain just when you and your

husband yearn for the intimacy necessary to make the adjustment to becoming a family. With another 'helping' person around, daddy can very easily feel that he's not much needed and drift into the habit of letting you and her, and then just you, get on with it.

Perhaps you have thought of having a nanny for a few weeks. Unless you plan to keep the nanny on indefinitely, or unless you are so ill that you can't look after the baby, having a nanny presents some of the same problems as your mother or mother-in-law, possibly even more. The nanny's job is only to look after the baby. She is an expert and therefore, although you may vaguely disagree with some of the nanny's notions, you are unlikely to argue, thus undermining your own confidence in looking after the baby. Because the nanny is there to look after the baby for the duration of her stay, you are unlikely to settle into the habit of caring for the baby yourself while she is there, and you might feel suddenly all at sea after she departs.

Also, unless you are bottle feeding, the nanny can't relieve you of the night feeds. The only advantage to having her is that she can look after the baby completely between feeds, thus affording you the chance to drop into bed to catch up on sleep with no worries about the baby. But so could an experienced babysitter.

Add to that the disadvantage that you would have a stranger as a house-guest, with whose likes and dislikes you are unacquainted and for whom you would have to cater at a time when you are really not up to coping with very much, either physically or emotionally. Remember, a nanny doesn't clean, shop, wash (except for the baby's nappies and clothes), iron or cook.

By this I don't mean that you shouldn't have any help. By all means, if you can possibly arrange it, do. But the best help to give you free rein with your new baby is for someone to come in during the day, or for a few hours during the day, to do the domestic chores, leaving you on own with your husband in the evenings, and I might add to that, someone of your own age or not much older so that you don't feel guilty watching them work.

If the new grannies live nearby, save yourself frustration by suggesting to them when is the best time of day, and even what days, to visit. Then you won't be surprised by visitors just when you've toppled into bed and just got the baby off to sleep. If they live some distance away, and are straining to visit their new grandchild, send them an instant photograph and suggest that *you* come to stay with them in a couple of weeks, which will give you an extended break from the cooking. If your mother or mother-in-law *must* come to stay with you, insist that they wait until you have been at home for at least a fortnight so that you have more or less got into a routine with the baby. Trying to establish a routine when you're very tired, with someone fluttering about being not particularly helpful, is much more difficult than if you are on your own.

Baby-sitting

Once you've got through the new baby stage, if your mother or mother-in-law lives nearby, the baby-sitting question arises. Will she,

or won't she? To anyone who has a willing granny, the question will seem laughable. But not every granny is eager to go through even a small share of child rearing again. I have one friend whose parents moved a couple of hundred miles to be near her and her husband when their grandchildren arrived, but not once has the granny ever offered either to babysit or to have them for a visit. Some women, after rearing their own offspring, feel that they've done their bit and want to get on with their own lives, which doesn't mean to say that they don't love their grandchildren and don't like to come and see them. Such was my friend's mother.

So unless granny eagerly offers, tread gently. Before announcing that you and your husband are going out and granny 'can come to sit with the baby', find out if she's willing, and make sure that she's physically up to it. Many older people don't like staying up late at night because they wake very early in the morning. If you are blessed with a willing granny, it is unkind to take advantage of her generosity, for she is doing you a favour. It's not much fun for her to come to babysit in the evening when the baby is most likely asleep. Babysitting is only enjoyable for her during the baby's waking hours.

This works both ways, of course. I have another friend where the granny considers her daughter-in-law to be very lucky to have her near, because she likes 'having the children'. The only trouble is that her daughter-in-law never knows in advance when granny is going to swoop in and carry them away for an hour or so. As a result, the daughter-in-law has to drop whatever she is doing and leap to take advantage of the opportunity that has suddenly dropped upon her. It is best for all concerned if there is some sort of flexible but regular arrangement, i.e. granny has the baby every Monday afternoon. That way a mother can plan to dash around the shops unencumbered, to do the ironing (a dangling iron cord is terribly dangerous after the baby can crawl), or go out to play tennis, once she has recovered her strength.

Still, if the granny in your family doesn't want to be tied down to a regular day or evening, then that's one of the perks of having got beyond the child rearing years, so it isn't fair to trespass on her freedom.

But neither should she trespass upon your arrangements for someone else to look after the children. Suppose you want to get away for a weekend or short holiday and there is someone who the baby or the children know and like who is available to look after them. Suppose in the first instance that granny has said that

she is unable, for whatever reason, to look after them herself —
she is too busy with other commitments, she feels that she isn't
up to it, whatever. It should be made adamantly clear to her before
you go that she should not interfere with the person who is looking
after them, and that she should only 'have the children' while you

are away at pre-arranged times, not just whenever she takes it into her head to drop in.

A substitute standing in for you at your home has enough to cope with in strange surroundings, working around the clock, without having to sort out granny. Furthermore, she is in a weak position to do so. Granny is 'family' and therefore related to her 'employer', so she has to listen. So if granny doesn't like how she is managing the children, the substitute hasn't a leg to stand on, even though she may be doing exactly what you want her to do, in precisely the way you want her to do it.

In these circumstances, granny must be told exactly when and for how long she can have the children while you are away, before you go. Otherwise, you have a formula for an overwrought child-minder and a tetchy granny: not a nice situation to come home to, and you'll never be able to go away and leave the children with that child-minder again.

Grandpa? Where is grandpa while all of this is going on? The answer, usually, is right there, unobstrusively enjoying every minute with his grandchild with never a word of advice. Funny, isn't it?

With Friends

A wise person, I wish I knew who, once said: 'The world is divided into two kinds of people — people who have children, and people who don't.' I shudder when I think back to the appalling midjudgements I used to make about people with children before I had them and began to understand.

I used to wonder for instance, why on earth a mother would drag small screeching children along on a shopping expedition. Answer: she had no one to leave them with and had to do the shopping, somehow.

I remember guiltily how I once descended as a house guest on a friend who had just come home from hospital with a new baby, and who stubbornly refused to let me help: I should have left immediately to lighten her burden.

I used to chuckle inwardly at what I considered to be parents' ambitions to educate their fairly young children, strolling through museums when obviously the children weren't interested. But it was the only way the *parents* could visit the museum, if they had no one to look after the children. The point I hope to drive home is how much having children, of necessity, changes the lives of their parents.

I remember once an old friend ringing from forty miles away, to announce that he and some friends were going to a pub near him, and could we meet them for lunch, an hour from then. We managed this, only just, having with difficulty got the telephone number of the pub to ring up and ask if there was a family room or a garden where we could park a pushchair (which wouldn't be too disruptive if its occupant decided not to like the pub). We heaped spare nappies, biscuits, and drinks of orange juice in a bag with assorted toys, and made off for nearly an hour's drive for the sedentary occupant of the child's safety seat, before she was asked to remain quiet and sedentary for yet *another* hour during our

lunch. We managed, rather tensely, to choke down lunch before the tot ran out of steam and patience. But you begin to see, I hope, just what is involved in trying to keep up some semblance of a normal friendship with childless friends.

It seems only too obvious when stated, but not so obvious before you go through the experience, that whenever you want to do anything with friends, as parents, first you have to arrange either how you will manage *with* the children if they are coming along, or how you can leave them.

If you manage to take them along, even successfully, a parent must always be busily making sure that the child is occupied and reasonably content. This, even before a baby can talk, involves a certain number of interruptions: to take the baby out if he cries, to change his nappy if it becomes soiled, to fish out the orange juice or biscuits to put off feeding him, to give him a breast-feed, to play with him to keep him amused, and to get him to bed when he is crying for a nap.

Once the baby can talk, and until he is old enough to learn that he mustn't interrupt, any adult conversation gets chopped into short telegraphic snippets between the baby's intrusions, and they are unavoidable. Few childless adults are sufficiently patient to pursue such interrupted conversations, and often can't understand why the mother doesn't 'teach the baby to be quiet'.

Childless friends who come to visit for the weekend suddenly find that both the mother and father have to look after the baby *all the time* — not much fun for a couple who want to be out and about, taking long walks over rough terrain over which the pushchair won't go (if the baby is too heavy to carry in a pack), dropping into quaint country pubs (already discussed), visiting stately homes (often too many stairs for prams or they are not allowed over fine carpets — not much fun for mum if she has to wait outside while the others go through).

Every excursion has to be carefully planned around the baby's sleeping and feeding pattern. Refusal to do so results at best in a whining infant, more often, in a loudly wailing tyrant.

Old and new friends

Most couples find that without great effort on both sides, childless friends tend to drift away. The interests of the new parents have to be channelled to child nurturing; their former friends retain all of their original adult interests. Add to that the fact that new parents usually have less money than before for leisure activities (usually only one pay cheque now and more out-goings), and it costs them more to go out if they have to pay a babysitter. Casual sports activities, for instance, such as football or squash which the couple may previously have gone to with friends, tend to slide away. Is it worth paying a babysitter and going to the trouble to book her, just to play squash, for a couple of hours, including the socializing afterwards?

If their friends are single, often their social activities are geared towards finding romance, a phase in which new parents have lost interest and the gulf stretches wider.

Most new parents find that having a child means finding new friends in much the same boat; even friends with children of more or less the same ages, so that they can co-ordinate their joint activities around similar schedules. For instance, if your child is still taking two daily naps, it isn't easy going for a day outing with

a couple whose two-year-old has given up naps altogether. A little later, parents may even find that four or five-year-olds almost need to be of the same sex or they don't get on very well. This might sound terribly restrictive, and there are naturally exceptions, but for daytime activities it is easier if your friends have the same logistical problems.

It seems unfortunate that just when new parents have so many other adjustments to make in their lives they tend to lose their oldest friends, and have to make an extra effort to make new ones. It happens, just when they are busier, more tired, and more home-oriented than ever before. Many couples I know simply cave in socially during the first two years of their first baby's life, and when they go out, go out alone as a couple. It's less hassle. But unless you come from a warm, extended family, living in the near vicinity, sooner or later you will find that you need friends. So where to find them?

Making new friends

The best way to find new friends is to look out for groups with similar interests. There you will meet people going through the same experiences as you.

The National Childbirth Trust is a country-wide organization whose primary function is to provide ante-natal classes and breast-feeding councillors. Although the Health Service provides ante-natal classes, those run by the NCT are very good and their breast-feeding councillors are often able to help a new mother through breast-feeding difficulties when otherwise she might have given up.

Apart from the excellent ante-natal classes, where mothers-to-be make friends with other expectant mums, who will all have their babies within a few months, the NCT has a network of support groups, of mum-and-baby and mum-and-toddler groups throughout the country, where new mothers get together socially.

Some groups meet in the daytime and bring their babies, some meet in the evening and bring breast-feeding babies, leaving older babies and toddlers at home with dad. The groups vary greatly. Some try always to have a speaker from outside to talk about a topic related to child rearing; others prefer an informal chin-wag. Most have mother-and-baby groups one morning or afternoon a week, where mothers bring their babies of whatever ages, and as the babies learn to sit up, they learn to socialize in different — and therefore interesting to the babies — environments. If the group is large, it may support a mother-and-baby group as well as a mother-and-toddler group. Some operate babysitting circles. Most meet in one another's houses, and therefore there is a chance to get acquainted in a relaxed informal atmosphere.

The National Housewives Register is an organization that sprang up to give women smothered in domesticity and child-rearing a chance to get out and talk about anything except children and domesticity. Again, members meet in one another's houses, sometimes for coffee mornings, sometimes in the evening. Usually a topic of discussion is decided in advance and one or two members do a bit of research to present an informal report to start off the discussion. Occasionally, there is an outside speaker. Some NHR groups also organize babysitting circles, trips to the theatre or concerts, to take advantage of special group bookings, and social evenings out. It is an excellent way for newcomers to an area to get acquainted.

When your child is a little older, usually about three, there are *playgroups* where mothers are drawn into a rota to assist the playgroup leader, as Social Services demand a ratio of one adult to every six or so children, the number depending upon the county in which you live. Many mothers find warm and lasting friendships develop not only through assisting in the playgroup, but through numerous fund-raising activities. The same may apply to local nursery schools.

The quickest way to find out if any of the above organizations have groups near you is to consult either your local library or Citizen's Advice Bureau, which keep lists of local organizations. This might, incidentally, yield other possibilities that may interest you, ranging from Friends of the Earth to the W.I. If none of these groups mentioned above are in your area, and you would like to start one, contact the national headquarters (addresses on page 173.) Also, don't forget any adult education classes that may be on offer, as these are an excellent, inexpensive, regular night out.

Parental competition

A note of caution: an odd competitiveness can often creep into the conversations between new mothers. Perhaps a chat starts quite innocently and impersonally, like a comment on the weather, with one mother asking the age of the other's baby. The first mother may respond by politely asking if the other's baby has any teeth yet, if he's started sleeping through the night, or begun to eat solid food.

Without thinking about it, it is terribly easy, in one's pride and delight with one's offspring, to begin to sound very proud and competitive, thereby making the other mother, whose offspring may scream three times every night to be fed, spit out solid food, and not have a tooth to show for it, feel more than a little bit defensive.

It's so easy, especially if you have no one to talk to about your baby's first — or fourth — tooth, or his almost word-like babble or singing, to crow about it to whoever happens on the scene. Almost invariably, it comes out sounding boastful, no matter what the original intent.

The opposite is the type of mother who complains about her baby's faults as though these faults are the biggest and best, hers the most trying baby on earth, and therefore by extension, she is the greatest martyred mum in the world.

It's funny when viewed from this distance, but if your best friend falls into the habit of opening every conversation with a question about whether or not your baby has sprouted any more teeth, with you knowing that she's just bursting to tell you that her baby has . . . well, it does get to be a bore, if nothing else.

Then there's the kind of mum who, when you start to discuss a problem that you are having with your child, concerning which you hope she might be able to give you a bit of homespun advice, responds with : 'Oh, I never had *that* kind of trouble with Peter.' This can make you feel about an inch high, thoroughly inadequate as a mother, and that you have unnecessarily exposed and somehow let down your dear little one in the bargain.

Now a word or two about 'earth mothers'. Oh yes, I've met them, how they like to go on and on about how much they enjoy their children, how they love including the children in their domestic chores, and how they feel that parenting a child is the most important thing they will ever do — at which point I feel like cringing, but that's just me . . .

There is no doubt that some women genuinely enjoy being with, playing with, doting over, and teaching, young children. Thank heavens that there are some who feel that way! Otherwise, who would become the nannies, the teachers in nursery schools, the leaders of playgroups, the infant and primary teachers? But even they are human.

In a good many cases even earth mothers, who start out set on having a family of at least six, quickly trim their sails to having no more than one or two after the first baby arrives and they are faced with the non-stop reality of rearing their own child. Fairly often, these same women who like to proclaim how utterly devoted their time and lives are to their children, if given a few minutes to rant, will wind down and start sounding remarkably like the rest of us, needing a bit of time off from the kids occasionally, like any other mortal mum. Who wouldn't?

Tolerance is the key word. All of us try in our different ways to be the best mothers we possibly can and often it is too easy to condemn anyone who sets out using a different set of rules.

The competitive element can get worse as the months and years go by. Some women, lacking any other creative outlet (and who has time for any?) knock themselves out collecting old boxes and cartons and snippets of this and that for at-home toddler craft sessions, and then tell everyone about it, showing what good mothers they are and making the rest of us feel that we are not giving our own children as much fun as some other mums.

Later on these same mums stay up all night baking surprise pretty-as-a-magazine picture birthday party teas for youngsters who would be happy with half the preparation and twice as many games or prizes. Believe me, young toddlers don't really enjoy birthday parties — only the bubbles and the balloons — unless they have an older brother or sister to egg them on to insist upon having a party.

The super-mum game is unending if you let yourself be sucked into it. If baking is your thing, if you really enjoy it and don't mind at all if most of the treats remain uneaten, go on and do the Beautiful Birthday Tea. If you enjoy sitting all morning making snowmen out of loo paper rolls, by all means, get on with it. But please, please, don't make the mother next door feel that she is an uncaring, undevoted, unloving mum because she can't stand the sight of a pair of scissors and a pot of glue, or if she can only just about manage to bake an instant cake.

Nothing kills a friendship between two mothers quicker than one making the other feel that she is somehow not a very good mother. We mothers are all in this together and need all of the moral support we can offer to one another during these demanding years: and we can help one another enormously. If you've got perfect pitch, try inviting the child of the wooden-eared mother next door over for your musical piano games with your toddler, and maybe she'll invite your child back when she's baking, or making paper fans . . .

If you show a large measure of tolerance and a sense of humour about what you may consider to be your friend's shortcomings, her returned tolerance will surely be welcome. Besides, your next child might be a horror like hers!

With Strangers

There is nothing like a bulge in the tummy region for bringing out, if not the worst in people, well — for bringing people out. Even people who are most reticent under normal circumstances will suddenly spy you across a room or in a supermarket and gallop over to offer advice as though they have known you for years. 'Wait a minute, dear, I'll open that heavy door for you.' 'Here, let me help you carry those bags, you really shouldn't try to carry such a lot of shopping in your condition.'

Most of the time this extra solicitousness on the part of perfect strangers, albeit surprising, is not altogether unpleasant, though it does on occasion seem intrusive: 'Got to eat for two now, haven't we, luv?' 'You really ought to give up smoking, you know, bad for the baby.' 'Now dear, you really shouldn't be wearing those spike heels while you're expecting, throws the spine out of line.'

It's as though simply because you have made the very personal decision to have a baby, you are suddenly thrust into the public domain. Old ladies who, the day before you donned your smock, would have determinedly elbowed you out of the bus queue, men who wouldn't have paid you the compliment of a glance, and women who under normal circumstances would never dream of passing more than a comment on the weather in a railway carriage, upon noting your condition feel that you need the benefit of some tender care and advice.

In the case of women, I suspect that it is because expecting and having a baby is so all-consuming an experience that those of us who have been through it remember that experience as one of such enormous consequence to our lives, that we therefore identify closely with anyone about to experience it. As for why men should take so much notice, I can't begin to fathom the Freudian nuances, if any. But there is no doubt about it, the sight of a pregnant woman brings out the chivalrous element in even the most brutish dolt of a man.

So enjoy it while it lasts. Once the bump is transferred to a pram or a pushchair, you usually have to fight your way through the crowds along the pavement again. And usually it's another woman who will offer to lift the pushchair up a flight of stairs or hold open a heavy door as you push the pram through.

Hospitals
In the medical world, this feeling of suddenly having thrust yourself body and soul into the public domain is hard to dispel, although ante-natal clinics and hospitals, sensitive to the criticism of treating women like so much sausage meat to be processed, try to make the whole infernal process a bit less inhuman.

It starts, generally, with a quiet confidential chat with your GP to ask for a pregnancy test, if you haven't already bought one yourself from the chemist. In any case, your first step is to inform your GP that you are expecting. Out come the forms, one which he gives you like a prize — the Certificate of Pregnancy — which relieves you from having to pay for any prescriptions while you are pregnant and for a year afterwards, and for free dental care during the pregnancy and for a year after. You'll probably be given a prescription for iron tablets, and a card with a printed schedule of appointments for ante-natal check-ups. These forms, while unavoidable, nevertheless can contribute to making you feel that you've just stepped onto a conveyor belt.

This feeling is reinforced by the regularity of ante-natal visits. Sometimes your GP will take your blood-pressure and prod your swelling tum, sometimes it's a midwife. If you live in an area where doctors advise their patients to have their babies in a hospital rather than in a maternity hospital, you'll be asked after three or four months, if it's practical, to continue your ante-natal visits to the hospital where much is made of your first visit, waiting to meet 'your' consultant. In the experience of most of the women I know, this was the first and last glimpse of 'their consultant'. On succeeding visits they were weighed, their blood-pressure was taken and their tums prodded by a procession of nurses, midwives and doctors who they rarely saw twice.

Despite realizing that all of this medical attention is for your own and your baby's welfare, it is very easy to feel as though the Establishment has taken you over in some sort of grand plan to protect the reproduction of the species and that your body is there to be examined and prodded by an army of medics, stripping away feelings of personal modesty and delicacy.

Looking back at my own pregnancies, it is difficult to think how the system could be altered and yet provide all of the safeguards that medical science now has to offer. It would be unreasonable to expect one or even two people to be able to take all of the blood-pressures, record all of the weight gains, make all of the blood tests, do all of the sonor scans as well as the abdominal examinations, internal and external, during the course of a pregnancy — and attend the delivery. For certainly it will be yet another midwife who will attend you during labour, or part of your labour. You might even succeed in having two midwives if one shift ends and another midwife takes over before your baby arrives!

To crown it all, if the baby is reluctant to slide gently through the birth canal and has to be helped with forceps — which usually means an episiotomy (a cut to enlarge the birth outlet) — a brand new face in the person of the docter on duty will come in to perform the cut, deliver your baby and stitch you up afterwards!

This is not a plea for the old days when women had their babies at home, tended by a midwife or doctor, although it might seem positively privileged to enjoy such privacy. There is no doubt that the facilities offered by modern hospitals to save you or your baby, if necessary, outweight this loss of privacy. But loss it is, and once having lost it in regard to one's body, rather like virginity, it's gone.

Child care experts

Another realm where strangers seem to intrude into your pregnancy and child-rearing, if you let them, is the realm of the experts — experts on television telling you how to potty train your toddler, experts writing in newspapers and women's magazines, experts writing books. Let me here and now disclaim any expertise with regard to having babies or bringing them on in the world. This book is being written as a long letter or chat from one friend to another — in fact it was first inspired by just such conversations with a friend who was trying to decide whether or not to have a baby — and I hope you will take it for just that. The ideas and opinions expressed are my own for you to read and accept — or toss to the wind. (So much for the short disclaimer.)

The daunting thing about reading what the experts suggest is that while much of it is very useful, the vastness of the subject matter can be overwhelming and, often, contradictory. Although this is not to say that you should not read any books on baby or child care. The comment of a friend of mine, who confessed that she knew so little about babies that she never put her baby down for a nap after he could crawl, and then wondered why he cried every afternoon, only shows that motherhood doesn't come all that naturally to a good many of us. We have to learn how to do it just like learning how to do anything else.

If there is no one to show you, and no ante-natal classes can possibly cram enough on baby care and child-rearing into a few sessions, you will have to find out some other way. Trial and error is not the quickest, most efficient method. Sometimes an idea you find in a baby book is so blindingly obvious that once you've read it, you wonder why on earth you never thought of it, but it has happened to me again and again. So it does help to look out for tips that others have found through experience to be useful.

Just keep an even keel, as they say in sailing, and sail through the deep waters of expertise with an eye to the wind of your own experience . . . as it comes.

PART II:
First Baby: Year One

8. Preparing for the Siege

A new mother's first few weeks at home with a new baby can be some of the happiest of her life. The following paragraphs were written soon after the arrival of our firstborn:

> We would stare deeply into one another's eyes for minutes stretched to small eternities, like two besotted lovers memorizing one another's faces. What did she see with those dark blue eyes, I wondered? Could she focus or was I merely a blur to her?
>
> The fixed, unblinking stare of a newborn babe can be rather unnerving. There is such a blank, all-seeing depth to their eyes, as though everything that passes before them is being indelibly etched somewhere on an empty slate of the mind, forever.
>
> Her gaze could have transfixed a sphinx. Had I not wanted her desperately, not loved her, if I had only been pretending, I felt that she would have seen straight through my falseness. It was like having a small omniscient monitor capable of winkling out any insincerity.
>
> It was good to have a baby in the dead of winter in that dreary lull after the holidays when spring seems unlikely ever to return. There was a special coziness in cosseting oneself indoors, looking out at a snowy landscape with no desire to set foot beyond the welcome mat, a babe in arms.
>
> I was never lonely, too tired perhaps. The mental, physical and emotional adjustment from a workaday world to a new 24-hour-a-day, 7-day-and-night, work-week took all of my concentrated energy.
>
> That there was so little time between feeds and my own meals, the laundry, a spot of ironing, occasionally, and if I were lucky, a short nap, was very difficult to accept at first. If I managed to skim a daily newspaper over lunch, or to make one telephone call during the day, I came to count myself well organized. It was just that tiny babies take a lot longer to eat than we do, and I hadn't reckoned on five hours of suckling a day.

Those first few weeks at home can be not only some of the

happiest of a woman's life, but some of the most trying, and
certainly, the most exhausting that she will ever have to face. So
prepare for the siege! *Anything* that you can do before the birth
to make your domestic life, and your husband's, run more smoothly
when you first come home from the maternity hospital, you will
be grateful for.

Household Stocking-up

The main reason for the great stock-up is to plan in advance the
easiest possible meals that you or your husband can prepare during
those first few weeks at home. You might even go so far as to plan
your meals on a two-week rota, writing it all down so that you don't
even have to think about what to have when the time comes.

Most women admit to feeling somewhat woozey as a result of
sleeplessness for quite a few weeks after the birth, so any effort
to think of what to eat, let alone preparing it, can seem rather a
burden. Although you may never ordinarily resort to convenience
foods, now is the time to throw principles to the wind and pile
up the packets and tins. Tinned and dehydrated foods keep for a
long time; if you have a freezer, pack in the frozen food.

Forget salads, unless your husband is a whiz at preparing them.
If there is time, it might give you a feeling of well-organized virtue
to freeze some home-made flans, casseroles, spaghetti sauce, pies,
cakes, or whatever. Stash the freezer full of an ample supply of chops
and chicken pieces, and remember that even sliced luncheon
meats, patés and salami, hard cheese, butter and margarine freeze
well, although eggs do not.

Before rushing out to the supermarket or freezer centre, draw
up several lists. Naturally, you will have to make your own, but here
are some ideas.

Staples: Cereals, rice, pearl or pot barley, jars of honey, marmalade
or jam, cooking oil, vinegar, soap powder, bars of soap, toothpaste,
shampoo, toilet paper, tissues, washing-up liquid, salt and pepper
and any other spices that you use frequently; and at least two
weeks' supply of sanitary napkins (for while you are bleeding,
because you won't want to use tampons for a while).
Lunches: Tinned or dried soups make excellent, quick lunches for
you, as do tinned fish, macaroni and cheese, or spaghetti, beans
on toast, etc.
Suppers: If you don't have a freezer, it will take a bit more ingenuity
to plan your six-week siege to provide interesting meals, as tinned

and dehydrated foods can get boring as a steady diet. But if you use them only three or four nights a week and have fresh food the others, it can relieve the tedium.

For instance, your husband or a neighbour might go shopping for you and buy a couple of portions of chicken, a couple of pork or lamp chops, or a packet of sausages every Saturday morning or on the supermarket's late night. A bacon joint is good, too, as it will keep for a few days before you need to cook it, enabling you to alternate fresh food with prepared, packet, or tinned food.

If your husband is going to take time off work for a few days to help out when you come home with the new baby, this forward planning will save either of you having to think about that eternal question — what's for dinner? He will only have to consult the menu and go out to buy such perishables as bread (if you have no freezer) and eggs (unless your milkman delivers them).

Do not, incidentally, waste these precious stores on your mother or your mother-in-law, if after soul searching you decide that you do want her to come and help out. She would undoubtedly prefer to cook what *she* plans rather than scrambling through your cupboards or freezer to find what you have on hand. It relieves you from having to remember where everything is to tell her, you won't need to think about the daily organization and, more importantly, it avoids possibly ruffling her feelings by telling her what to do.

Let her go shopping with your husband and leave the decisions — and the cooking — to her while she is there, and save your happy hoard for her departure when you and your husband are really on your own.

Household Laundry

Another way to lighten your load during the first few weeks at home — bearing in mind that a new baby can use from six to twelve nappies a day — is to arrange either to send your bedding out to a laundry for a while if you don't have a drier, or to get your husband to drop it into a launderette where he can leave it to be done. Without a drier, or a large warm place somewhere inside where washing can dry, drying the nappies can be enough of a problem without having sheets draped over everything, not to mention what it can do to your morale.

Another energy saver is for you and your husband, as much as possible, to wear no-iron clothes for at least those first six weeks. If your husband *must* wear ironed shirts, explain to him that you won't be physically up to it, and either he will have to iron his shirts for a while or send them out to a laundry. Of course, if you hire someone to clean, perhaps that person could do a bit of necessary ironing as well.

Make-Up, Clothes and Hair

To avoid having to go out shopping during those first few weeks at home, stock up on any make-up or cosmetics that you think you may need. A nice bottle of bath oil or bubble bath wouldn't go amiss to help you to feel more glamorous! If the budget will stand it, it is also nice to have a couple of new casual outfits to look forward to wearing after months in maternity clothes. Choose clothes that are fairly loose fitting and, if you plan to breast-feed, ones that either open down the front, or tops that can easily be lifted up and tucked in.

Do get your hair styled before the baby comes, in a style that is easy to look after as well as attractive. This doesn't have to mean short or straight. A soft perm on medium-length hair looks good — a bolster to a sagging ego — and only requires shampooing once a week (and no setting), whereas a straight, blunt cut may need more frequent shampooing.

Just a warning: sometimes a perm won't 'take' during the last few weeks of pregnancy. Get advice about this from your hairdresser. But I cannot urge you enough to have your hair styled or trimmed before the baby is due. It is so much easier to pop into a salon unencumbered by a pram. Even if the baby were to continue to sleep, you wouldn't be at ease, wondering if he were going to wake up at any moment. If he did and wanted to be fed at just the wrong time, it could be embarassingly disruptive, and if you were breast-feeding, downright awkward, not to mention catastrophic for the timing of your perm.

Feeding

As the method of feeding you choose will determine the equipment you will need, let me digress from the forward planning for a moment to discuss breast versus bottle, and mixed feeding.

Even with hindsight, and considering all of the disadvantages, I would breast-feed again. Apart from the fact that it is best for the baby, other advantages are that you do not need to sterilize bottles (except for drinks of water, and later, orange juice), you save the time you would otherwise have spent mixing feeds, and you don't have to pack them wherever you go. The baby's milk is always with you, ready, if you can find a quiet and private corner.

The disadvantages are that you, the mother, from the moment the baby is born, are tied by an invisible umbilical cord to the baby's feeds, every four hours theoretically, more likely every three hours. If you are extremely unlucky, it can even be every two hours, sometimes, day and night. Night feeds may go on for as little as ten days, three or four weeks, six weeks, or more often, until the baby is ready for solid food at about four months. But not always — it might be much longer.

At first glance, if you choose to breast-feed, poor 'participating dad' is pretty much cut out of the proceedings. But he *could* give the baby a feed, preferably a night feed, if he will agree, if you are sufficiently patient to use a breast pump to dribble enough milk out. However, the women I know who have used a breast pump have all lost patience after two or three attempts because it takes so long to extract two or three ounces of milk).

If you manage to get the baby on to what I call 'mixed feeding', part breast-feeding and part bottle-feeding (mixed feeding as referred to by the medical profession usually means some kind of milk and solid food), your husband could certainly give the baby at least one bottle during the night, to give you a chance to sleep through six or seven hours without a break — provided you are a sufficiently heavy sleeper not to wake up when the baby cries! Getting the baby to take an occasional bottle also means that you are free to go out. You can leave a bottle with someone else to give to the baby.

Most women, however, seem to settle on one method or the other, breast-feeding or bottle-feeding. Should you decide to breast-feed, you can count on losing up to two or three hours of sleep out of every night for a period of twelve to sixteen weeks, and that adds up to a lot of lost sleep, especially at a time when you are already at a low physical ebb after the birth. So making the rest of your life as easy as possible is wise . . . the night feeds don't last forever!

Stock-Up for the Baby

In theory, if you breast-feed, you should need only one or two small bottles for drinks of water, and later, orange juice, a bottle brush, and a sterilizing kit, although a large covered plastic canister will do as well, or you can always sterilize by boiling (Check directions on plastic bottles.) Having said that, my breast-fed babies refused to take water altogether after the first three days, during which I think the younger would have consumed anything put near his mouth. It was several months before either would take diluted orange juice.

If you plan to do mixed feeding, part breast-feeding and part bottle-feeding, you will need two or three large bottles as well, plus the sterilizing kit, the bottle brush, and several weeks' supply of sterilizing tablets to drop in. It is practical to find out what formula the maternity hospital uses, if your baby is put on one there, so that you can continue it at home to avoid possible upset caused by a change.

If you are planning to bottle-feed exclusively, most baby books say that you will need at least nine or ten bottles and, of course, the sterilizing kit, a bottle brush, and sterilizing tablets.

Even if you breast-feed, you will eventually need two or three large bottles for after weaning the baby to cow's milk (anything after six months), that is, if you don't wean the baby straight on to a snorkel cup. Some babies will; mine wouldn't.

Double check to make sure that you have the last minute items, besides the baby clothes and equipment mentioned earlier.

You will need a couple of large jars of cream for the baby's bottom (zinc and castor oil or vaseline, or one of each); cotton swabs for cleaning the baby's ears and nose (new babies are often snuffly); cotton balls for wiping and washing down the baby's bottom, washing behind his ears, and in the creases around pudgy neck and groins (though you can use a flannel); sterilizing powder for soaking nappies; and about two dozen cloth nappy liners or several packets of disposable liners (to throw away after bowel movements or wash when wet only). You may consider using disposable nappies for the first few weeks, almost certainly if you have a Caesarean. Without doubt, disposables are easier than washing nappies but, in the long run, more expensive than terries. Don't risk a plugged drain by trying to flush disposables through the plumbing. It is better to throw them out with the rubbish, in plastic bags to avoid a pong.

The main disadvantages to disposables is the expense. Also the edges of the plastic may irritate the baby's legs, and sometimes urine seeps out through the too-large leg holes if you happen to have a tiny baby. Disposables can come unstuck as well, wetting the cot (more bedding to wash), and wasting that particular nappy. (It is best to buy disposable nappies after the birth, in case you have a large baby who won't fit size one.)

House Cleaning

If you happen to be reading this in the highly inflated later stages if pregnancy, you may laugh when I suggest that now is the time to clean your house. By that I don't mean to get down on your hands and knees to scrub or to climb any ladders to wash windows. But now is the time to clear out every drawer, shelf and cupboard of clutter — dusting, wiping and washing as you go.

If the house is clean and tidy before you go to the maternity hospital, then when you come home with the baby, although the surface dust may have accumulated during your absence, at least you will have the peace of mind to know that everything else is in order. Believe me, after the baby arrives, and then perhaps if yet another baby arrives, — you won't have another chance to do this kind of thorough cleaning out for a very long time.

For a normally fastidious woman, having to let her normal cleaning go by the board is hard enough. When the untidiness starts to build up, resulting in simply sticking this and that into drawers and cupboards (if they are not already reasonably orderly), then in only a short time she can feel that she is fighting an endless battle against clutter, or even chaos. Such a state is not conducive to making her feel that she is on top of the world, it is far more likely to make her feel harrassed, guilty and depressed.

Recall that lovely moment when the house is just freshly cleaned and looking its best. It may be fleeting, but at least you have the pleasure of knowing how nice it can look. The same applies to the insides of drawers, cupboards, and wardrobes. It's your inner peace at stake, not some grand gesture to Good Housekeeping.

Besides, it helps to pass those last dragging days before the baby arrives. Most women find that they tire rather easily during the last few weeks of pregnancy, so the best plot is to do only one kitchen cupboard a day, for instance, or one wardrobe, or one chest of drawers, and if the baby is late and you run out of drawers, it's a good time for visiting friends who live nearby, or dipping into those still unread novels in the bookcase — and more than one Last Meal Out has seemingly started a reluctant lump on its way!

9. The Emotional Everest

'Her arrival, when at last it came, was very welcome, as only arrival of a firstborn child, born just inside the boundary of childbearing years, eight days late and after two sleepless nights, can be.

'Labour had gone on so long that subconsciously, my husband and I had almost despaired of her ever appearing. We had hoped to smooth her birth with the lowered lights and quiet voices of the Leboyer method, leaving her umbilical cord to pulsate until she had gulped those first few all important breaths of air.

'But regrettably, the last stage of labour was prolonged, and she had to be strongly yanked from her warm, cozy passageway with forceps, and the cord chopped abruptly from around her neck.

'I shall never, ever, forget that awful sound, like a pair of secateurs severing a particularly tenacious branch, and that dreadful moment of silence before she let out an angry cry. Oh, the relief of it — she was alive — inside my heart seemed to explode.

'Somewhere an emotional dam burst, sending out waves of warmth. I felt touched to the very core, as though a giant finger had prodded my heart. Not even our wedding, which had left my knees shaking uncontrollably, had moved me to such depths.

'Though we had been looking forward to, preparing for, and getting used to the idea of having a child for more than nine months, and though labour had been agonizingly long, still, the instant of birth arrived suddenly, the peak, the climax of all the worry, waiting and pain.

'The world changed in a twinkling. At no time had my life ever flared so dramatically in a second.

'One moment, we were just the two of us, pushing and straining. Then there she was, beet red, screaming, her little chin trembling miserably, her tiny arms flailing out in alarm, fists clinched, her little legs folded in a bow across her tummy as she had lain in the womb.

'My husband and I were so relieved; but such a pathetic little mite she looked. Her father instinctively reached out to take her from the midwife's arms. He stood, cradling her in one large hand against his white hospital gown, his other hand in mine, as the tears streamed down our faces.

'Of course, even then, any number of things could have been wrong with her, might be still. But that she had all her fingers and toes, that she could open her eyes and make a noise, that she seemed to be "all right" — screaming with rage at her sudden catapult into this bright, noisy alien world — was very reassuring.

'Two hours later when they brought her to me, still in the dark of a wintry dawn, I was too weary to move. Her presence was no more than a small warm spot and a tiny nibbling at the breast through the weight of my fatigue.

'I think it was then that it hit me like a monstrous wave; no day, no night, would ever again be the same. There would always be this small person ceaselessly demanding to be held and fed, loved and cared for. How different life was from only two hours before.

'At that moment, the irrevocable relentlessness of it made me feel quite tired, not up to it. Yet at the same time, despite the fatigue, I felt exhilarated and euphoric. Even after two nights without sleep, I couldn't sleep. She was here, at last.

'As the light rose I could hardly tear my eyes from the tiny dark-haired head clearly visible through the clear perspex crib. My eyes kept welling full of tears. She seemed so tiny, so vulnerable, so dependent. Our child. And what an alarming variety of noises she made — squeaks, snuffly breathing, snorts, sneezes, hiccups, and that rhythmic crying of the newborn in short bursts that I quickly came to recognize as — "Help, help! I'm starving."

'Each time I picked her up I was struck anew by her tender fragility, by the wonder that all of her miniscule fingers, none more than an inch long, and her lentil-sized finger and toenails should be so exquisitely formed.

'It seemed unbelievable that so tiny a being could be perfect, so complete. Each tiny arm fully extended fitted snugly into one of my hands; each ear was the size of my thumbnail. Her plump little bottom rested easily in one palm, and prying her tiny toes apart to wash them, my fingers felt like thick blunt objects. How delicate she was.

'Awake she had the wide, slightly squint-eyed stare of a young kitten, still vaguely startled at discovering itself alive. Nuzzled into the breast, her eyes would half close in a swoon. It always made me sigh with pleasure to think that I could give her this comfort.

'From that first day, lying on her tummy, she could hold her head up herself. We were immensely pleased and proud; it meant that she was strong. All those pints of milk, iron tablets and floride pills had been worthwhile.

'My eyes kept filling with tears of gratitude that she had been born "all right", that fate had allowed this so precious bundle to be delivered undamaged.

'The theme of Sigfried's Idyll, that ethereal serenade composed by Wagner for his wife Cosima on the first birthday of their little son, came wafting out over the radio during breakfast the second morning after her birth.

'I have always found it poignantly touching — Wagner seems to have had his secret ear tuned to the angels — but for the first time I began to understand the deep, strong and tender bond between two people who have created a child.

'I did a lot of crying those first few days, not tears of sadness but tears of overflowing joy. I was touched afresh by each arrival of flowers, cards and telegrams from friends and relatives, with each gift of a doll-sized sweater, tiny cap or bootees.

'Other people seemed to appreciate the emotional pinnacle we had scaled. *Why had no one told us what to expect?* One gets so much advice about what will happen medically and clinically, but there had been no hint of the explosion within, opening into a deeper-hued expanse of emotional landscape.

'Admittedly I am sentimental — I cry at movies and sad novels — though most of my friends see only a matter-of-fact, vaguely cynical veneer. Suddenly, the veneer had melted. I felt exposed, naked and vulnerably adrift in a sea of emotions, a warm and happy sea to be sure, but nevertheless, disconcertingly out of control.

'Part of it, doubtless, was physical. Exhaustion and pain stripped away pretense. Merely to move from one room to another was an almost unendurable journey of pain, and I could scarcely bare to sit, even on a pillow, thanks to countless stitches. Yet even through this dense thicket of weariness and pain, I was flushed with happiness.

'The world seemed a very different place than it had before. Colours and emotions were more intense, music seemed more touchingly beautiful. It was as though I had suddenly tuned into a different wave length, at a high frequency of beauty, at an intense passion of artistic creativity, where the best endeavours of mankind are achieved. It was like being buoyed up by a new system of harmony composed to a splendid, more natural and satisfying melodic scale tuned to the tides and the planets.'

But to suggest that *every* woman shares this kind of birth experience would be less than honest. Many women feel absolutely nothing at all towards the baby for quite a long time. Even the same woman, giving birth a second time, can have a very different experience emotionally, as witness the following, written soon after the birth of our second child:

'Bless him, at least he did the decent thing by starting his journey at 5.00 in the morning, so that we didn't lose a night's sleep during labour.

'The labour was progressing well, so well that by mid-morning, we thought that he would be with us within the hour. But no. The labour went on and on. By 2.00 in the afternoon, I was beseeching them to do a Caesarean.

' "The baby would be here before we got you ready," they said. But he wasn't.

'It was just after 4.00 that they decided to use forceps. By then, I only wanted it to be over and done. So when the midwife chuckled, calling him a baby elephant as he came out, I thought she was joking, until she put him on the scales and announced that his birth weight was ten pounds and seven ounces!

'When she held him up for my husband and me to see, bellowing his head off, plum purple, his puffy eyes tightly shut, his fat jowly face screwed up in an outrage, his dark wet hair stuck to his head, he was not a pretty sight. He was downright ugly — Mr. Magoo or Winston Churchill minus the cigar on a very bad day.

'When the midwife put him to my breast, he bit me so hard that I nearly shot off the table. Surely he had teeth?

'My husband looked at me questioningly, and we both burst out laughing. Could he be ours? He *had* to be ours, well, a boy would be different. There was none of the heart-touching, tear-drenching solicitude for the miserable little mite our daughter had seemed when she was born.

'This was no fragile mite. This fat bundle, his chubby arms and legs jabbing like a wrestler, was a chap to be reckoned with.

'What had we let ourselves in for, I wondered?

' "He was a very hungry big boy," said the nurse who took him away for the usual tests and brought him back sated with milk and glucose. Mercifully, I was allowed a good sleep that first night.

'During the next two days he bellowed a good deal. He was, indeed, a hungry boy, and I allowed him to suckle as long as I dared in the hope that he might bring in the milk early.

'To my relief and his, my breasts began to swell the second day. He was desperately hungry. Every couple of hours he cried, so much that the poor mother in the next bed was fraught with being awakened so often during the night, and the baby elephant had to go to the "naughty room" more than once during our stay at the maternity home so that both she and I could get some sleep.

'Would I ever love him even half as much as our little girl, I asked myself, as I stared down at his fat, ruddy little face, floating in rings of double chins?

'It was three days before he opened his eyes for more than a flutter. In the wee hours of one night, a sudden fear jabbed me. What if he were blind?

'Somehow I managed to control my hysterical fear until the next morning when I tried, casually, to ask the doctor if his eyes were all right.

' "Oh yes," he assured me. "But the pressure of the birth has caused some swelling and that will take a few days to go down."

'Looking back, I think that was probably the beginning of maternal concern.

'When the swelling did go down, one eye was gooey, which didn't add any charm to his general appearance, and he continued to frown ferociously. I tried drawing the curtains to lessen the light, but that didn't seem to matter.

'Would he ever settle into a happy, contented baby, as his sister had been, I wondered? Or was this the beginning of an unbridled fury that would torment us through toddlerhood — not the sort of thoughts to elicit warm feelings of tenderness and solicitude.

'Not even when he nestled into the breast, the only time *he* looked reasonably placid, did *I* feel any rush of emotional tides.

'Looking back, I think that my *positive* feelings for the baby only began to flutter when at last the rashes started to disappear, the eye stopped oozing, his plum colour softened to peach, and he went down to four feeds a day and one at night, which meant that not only did he *look* a bit better, but I was not quite so tired. Or as my husband put it, the baby "began to look not so bad that you couldn't take him out!" '

If you are trying to decide whether or not to have a child, I hope you won't have been put off reading the rest of the book by these birth experiences. The decision to treat you to some of the emotional reactions was quite deliberate, because up until now I have not read descriptions of the emotional highs (and lack of them) that mothers experience. Most books deal only with the medical aspects of pregnancy and birth, leaving emotional responses to accidental discovery. Naturally, I can't forecast how you, personally, might respond, but it would have been nice to know, I think in retrospect, what might lie ahead, how others have felt.

10. How Fathers Can Help

After the flowers and the chocolates and the scenes of elation at the maternity hospital, during those few days before a new mother comes home with the new baby, when a father's only contribution has been to cook and look after himself — no mean task for some men — and to pop in at visiting hours; after this little lull, during which he may well be looking forward to his wife getting home so that she can look after *him*, that is when fatherhood really begins. Rarely is it any less of a shock to a man than motherhood to a woman.

Suddenly, the mother and baby are at home, but she is not her usual energetic self. It is likely that her husband is accustomed to leaving work and coming home to relax in the evening. But now that he is a father, he will simply have to help out at home. Parenting goes on day and night and any woman who tries to carry the whole load by herself risks sinking lower and lower, and taking much longer to regain her strength.

It would be ideal if every new father could take three or four weeks 'paternity leave' so that he and his wife, upon her homecoming from the maternity hospital, could settle into parenthood together. By sharing parenthood round-the-clock for even a few weeks, fathers would become aware of how much time and work are involved just in looking after a new baby, plus even a minimum of housekeeping. Given a chance, most fathers these days would probably welcome the opportunity to have more intimate contact with their newborn babies. It is just that if their only opportunity is at the end of a tiring work day, or at weekends when other household tasks need to be done, not much child nurturing gets fitted in. It is much better if a father learns to care for his new baby together with his wife. This is a very special time, when a couple first become parents, and an experience that is much more pleasurable if shared. To do so is to face a major adjustment united, together. Not to do so, inevitably, will result in the father not understanding nearly so well what the mother is doing all day, and possibly, not being as sympathetic to her needs or to those of the baby.

Even with paternity leave, soon enough the mother will most probably have to adjust to carrying the major load of the child care. But there are ways that a considerate husband can help, and which require very little effort on his part.

Punctuality to the Rescue

To keep a new mother tip-top emotionally during this period, one of the most important, though seemingly small, things that a husband can do is to come home punctually, when expected. Women seem to suffer from sudden drops in energy during those first few weeks after the baby's arrival. At eleven o'clock in the morning a mother may be on top of the world, thinking that she has everything in hand. But by 4.00 or 4.30 it can suddenly hit her like a sack of potatoes thrown over her back — a weight of tiredness almost too heavy to be endured. Unfortunately, this is usually when the baby wants a feed, to be changed, and the supper started, all at the same time.

If a father can stride through the door, sympathetic and soothing, to give her a cuddle and to take the baby off her hands and up to bed — although almost invariably babies decide to be wakeful just when supper needs to be prepared — he can rescue a day from taking a dramatic downward plunge.

Just knowing that he'll be coming can sometimes keep a woman going for another quarter of an hour. If he's late, even by only a few minutes, it can sometimes push an already hard-pressed mother past the breaking point, turning what might have remained a fairly successful, happy day with a timely rescue at the end of it, into a day when she went to pieces, ending in tears.

New mothers *are* precariously balanced emotionally — all of us, even the most level headed at others times — during this period when the hormones are making drastic adjustments after having given birth. So there is no need to be too hard on yourself. Simply accept it as normal, explain why to your husband and plead for his understanding, suggesting specific ways in which he can be helpful. Remember that it's a whole new world to him, too, and you will probably be getting more practice at baby-minding than he is. So you mustn't leap down his throat if you have to show him half a dozen times how to fold a nappy.

Those first six weeks or so are a siege. Facing them together as new parents can cement and strengthen your relationship. Without your husband's help and loving support, those first few weeks with a new baby can be a nightmare. Also, if you do not face this crisis together it may establish a pattern, and a crack, in your marriage as your husband leaves you to get on with looking after the baby on your own.

It might give both of you some consolation to consider that if a woman were just coming out of hospital after an illness or an operation and she took on a brand new, physically and emotionally demanding job, working fourteen to eighteen hours a day, seven days a week, with no more than six hours of sleep a night, and that broken every three hours . . . everyone around her would say that she was mad, and that to succeed at the job under such conditions would be impossible. Well, welcome to motherhood!

Baby Care

A mother will probably have to teach her husband how to care for the baby, just as she was taught in the maternity hospital. Otherwise, her husband won't know how to help out. Settling into a routine at home together, not only lightens the load on the mother, but enables the father, at last, to begin to feel that he, too, is involved in the business of parenthood.

As I have already said, *short of breast-feeding, a father can do anything for his child that a mother can*. He might empty the nappy pail into the washing machine, fill up the bucket again with nappy soaking solution and return it to wherever the nappies are changed, each morning, saving the mother from carrying a heavy bucket too soon. He might prepare breakfast for himself and his wife while she is giving the baby a breast-feed, if it comes just before breakfast. If the early morning feed falls so that it is best for the mother to have a late lie-in instead of getting up for breakfast together, he could sometimes prepare the day's formula if she is bottle-feeding.

Of course, he can cuddle the baby, dress or undress him, change his nappy, remake his carrycot, bath him, play and chat with him and take him for walks. In the evening when he gets home from work, a father might either start the supper (or watch that it doesn't go up in smoke) while the mother gives the baby a feed. Even if a husband lacks distinction in the culinary department, at least he ought to be able to heat up a tinned meat pie, or plop a couple of chops under the grill, and open some tinned or frozen vegetables. (Better still if finances will stand it, he might occasionally bring home fish and chips, take-away Chinese, or best of all, take his wife out to a pub for a quick meal. Hopefully, a neighbour or a friend might babysit for an hour — remember those unpredictable feeds?)

The mother and father might also share in giving the baby a late-day bath. Once the baby has had his feed (and bath), the father might dress him in his night clothes and tuck him in while his wife is taking up the supper. The father might, just occasionally, interrupt his own supper to go up and see why the baby is crying, whether he had kicked the covers off, got the hiccups, or needs a nappy changed. He might even, sometimes, drag himself out of bed to see why the baby is wailing during the night, if he knows that his wife has just given the baby a (breast-)feed an hour ago, or he could give the baby a bottle-feed himself, now and again, so that his wife can sleep through uninterruptedly.

Shopping

If you follow my advice, there should be very little or no shopping during the first six weeks that you are home from the maternity hospital, but whatever shopping there is should be done by your husband, a friend or a neighbour, unless you are really yearning for some fresh air. If you are, let your husband push the pram or heave the carrycot in and out of the car, and avoid lifting heavy grocery bags. Don't feel guilty about conserving what energy you have.

Cleaning

During your first few weeks at home, forget house cleaning and ironing. Any spare time should be reserved to sink into bed to sleep with the telephone off the hook and a note on the doorbell to discourage callers. The house cleaning will keep, or if you and your husband feel that it won't, this problem should be resolved long before you are hauled off to the delivery room.

Just how thoughtful and helpful is your husband?

If you are not feeling well, does he get out the vacuum cleaner at the weekend and do a trek around? Does he carry out the rubbish from the pedal bin (while you are heavily pregnant), just to save you a few steps? Would he iron a shirt if he realized that you weren't up to it? Or is he the sort who feels that it is his divine right to come home to such an immaculate house, courtesy of his wife, that it would take a Mrs Ogmore-Prichard to satisfy him: 'And before you let the sun in, mind it wipes its shoes.' (*Under Milk Wood* by Dylan Thomas).

If he is so fastidious that he couldn't abide letting things go for a while, work out some solution as to how to maintain standards — by his helping out or hiring help — at least until the baby starts sleeping through the night, and you have a chance to recover some of your energy. This is important because every spare moment during those first few weeks and often months, if the baby continues to wake for night feeds, you will desperately need to rest in order to catch up the two or three hours of sleep that you will be missing every night! If you don't, you will simply grow more and more tired, and sink into a downward spiral of exhaustion, impatience, short-temper, and eventually become depressed . . . and incidentally, you will not be a very nice person to be around!

With your husband's co-operation in caring for the baby and in giving you a hand with the domestic chores — and if both of you relax your usual standards of housekeeping and cooking for the duration of the night feeds — you *can* enjoy your new baby, even through the haze of a yawn. . .

11. The First Four Months

Cheer up! Once the first few days after the baby's birth have passed, when your knees feel like jelly whenever you try to stand, your breasts balloon out like Marilyn Monroe (if you are breast-feeding), after you have blubbed through the third morning blues and had your stitches removed (if you have any, and if they are not self-dissolving), *then* you can begin to chart your daily rising of sap from the rock bottom of limp euphoria immediately after the birth, to a week or so later when you begin to get fidgety to get home.

Although you may well become impatient to leave the maternity hospital before the end of the customary ten days, once home, you will almost certainly experience a feeling of lead-heaviness, not unlike the last few weeks of pregnancy, whenever you try to get up out of a chair. Fear not, this is sheer weariness and it will go away in time.

Even a friend of mine who had the good fortune to have a thirty-minute labour, from the breaking of the waters to the appearance of her baby boy, felt extremely tired when she got home with her new baby, having to get up two or three times every night to feed him. If labour lasts longer, if the baby is born in the small hours, making you lose a night's sleep, or if it is a Caesarean delivery, your strength will sink lower, and it will naturally take longer to recover.

It is well known that one of the most effective tortures to break down a prisoner is to keep him constantly awake, or to let him have no more than an hour's sleep at a time. Only slightly less extreme is the pattern of sleeplessness that most mothers of newborn babies endure; at best they rarely get more than four hours of sleep at a stretch for a while.

During our first night home with our firstborn we had a terrible fright. Waking in the morning, we realized that she had gone through the night without a feed — at ten days old! Stricken with guilt for fear that we had slept through her crying, and terrified at what we might find, hand in hand, my husband and I tiptoed into her room. To our immense joy, at hearing a noise her little bottom started bouncing up and down under the covers.

Even at ten days old, her character was beginning to show itself. The sight of her tiny booteed feet sticking out from under her gown, kicking up and down, never failed to make us laugh. The indignant kicking always accompanied the five minues or so of grumble-crying before she abruptly dropped off to sleep, just long enough to let us know how wrong we were about putting her down.

We were fortunate. From the time we arrived home, she gave up the early morning feed and was satisfied with breakfast anytime after 8.00! The night feed fell sometime between one and four. I used to groan inwardly at the first sound of her rhythmic crying amplified over the baby alarm. It seemed too much to ask of any human being, especially me, leaden with fatigue, to have to rise in the middle of a January night in a chill house to grope for a dressing gown and slippers to pad across the corridor.

But without exception, when I got there, turned on the fan heater, poured myself a cup of warm milk from the thermos, lifted her out of her crib and nestled her to the breast, the irritation and tiredness would flee. The contentment of that small, warm being transmitted itself to me like the soothing warmth of a hot water bottle. Sometimes during that feed I would think that we were closer than at any other time. The house was quiet, no dogs barked, no birds sang. There was only she and me, close, together. Somehow I can't imagine that bottle feeding could possibly give the same feeling of tender, warm intimacy as a snuggly baby, cuddled to the breast.

Most of the time, she was an extremely happy baby. Each morning she woke herself with gurgles and cooings. As I bent over the crib to turn her onto her back, she would greet me with a big radiant smile, her whole face beaming, all arms and legs kicking, instantly transforming a grey morning for a weary mother into a bright, brilliant new day full of joy and hope and loving.

During the day, I remember all too well the burden of tiredness that seemed to hang over my shoulders like a heavy shawl. To lift myself out of a chair and make a cup of tea sometimes seemed almost too much of an effort. Added to the soreness in the vaginal area caused by the stitches of an episiotomy healing, which made any sitting position painful — and pain is wearing — I was vaguely demoralized. Why wasn't I one of the glowing mums on the packet of disposable nappies, instead of the sallow hag who stared back at me from the mirror? If you feel like that, well, no need to worry. I soon discovered that nearly everyone feels a bit like that! Just accept being tired as normal and get as much rest as possible.

Perhaps the most useful bit of advice ever given to me was by a mother of a baby and toddler who said: 'You've got to stay completely flexible, ready to drop whatever you're doing at any time, no matter what, whenever a child needs you. You just have to resign yourself to the fact that *your time is no longer your own*.' This is true, I might add, *day or night*.

Flexibility is precisely the word, especially in those early weeks and months. Whenever the baby is hungry, whenever the baby wakes up, a mother has to be ready to jump and drop everything. That doesn't sound unreasonable until you start to think about the various other tasks that you have to accomplish along with looking after the infant.

The baby's nappies and bedding, if you are lucky, pop into an automatic washing machine and only take five minutes to hang up when they come out, but there is the inevitable hand washing. If you feel a bit more ambitious, preparing a casserole or baking a cake can go disastrously wrong if the baby decides to sleep for only thirty minutes when you were counting on at least an hour to get something into the oven. Or it can be very disheartening to hear a tiny wailing from upstairs just when you have dropped off to sleep for that afternoon snooze you so badly need.

What I found so difficult to grasp at the time and, I dare say, what will probably be hard for you until you are faced with the reality of motherhood, is just *how* flexible you really must be.

You may think that your baby is settling into some sort of feeding pattern just when the baby ups and moves onto another pattern. Some babies start sleeping through the night at five or six weeks old — some even earlier — and never disturb your slumber thereafter. Others may continue to wake up two, or even three, times a night throughout their first year, or even longer.

Neither is it possible to guess how long a baby is going to sleep between feeds during the day. It might be only half an hour before a baby wakes up after a feed, wanting something, or it may be four hours, three hours, or only two hours. If only we could wind them up like alarms or put in our specifications in advance. But neither have the babies any choice of parents, so I suppose that we are all in this Russian roulette of happy families together.

The best attitude to take is that of simply rolling with it, not trying to plan very many unnecessary tasks, and never thinking that anything can be accomplished quite as quickly as it was before — pre-baby. If you adopt what Americans call a 'laid-back' philosophy, life will be a lot more pleasant than if you stew yourself into trying to do too much, too quickly.

A Flexible Framework

Despite the total unpredictability of a baby, it may be helpful to have some sort of rough framework to work around or you can easily find yourself still in your dressing gown at five o'clock in the evening — not that it matters except to your morale — or with no dry nappies when you reach for a clean one (it is never a bad idea to keep a packet of disposables on hand, just in case you run out if you have difficulties with drying space).

But trying to keep yourself or the baby to any schedule during the first two or three weeks home from the maternity hospital, unless you have what is called an easy baby — one who eats fairly regularly and sleeps sweetly for most of the time in between — will be very nearly impossible; so don't worry about it. The thing to remember is that only a few things really have to be done every day, and the rest, if possible, fitted in around them.

Imperatives — Feeding the baby
— Washing and drying nappies, baby clothes and baby's bedding.
— Preparing and eating your own meals
— Catching up on sleep
Secondary — Bathing the baby
— Washing the dishes
— Arranging for your own bed linen and clothes to be laundered and ironed, weekly or fortnightly
— Tidying the house (forget real cleaning)

Listed like this you may wonder, why all the fuss? You'll have bags of time. But you won't.

Start with feeding the baby. Having read the baby books that suggest giving the baby ten minutes on each breast, you might jump to the obvious conclusion that a feed will take only a total of twenty minutes. But by the time the baby may have fallen asleep once or twice during the feed, you have changed his nappy once or twice, and possibly his bed, and winded him, which is often slow, you can usually count on a feed taking at least an hour.

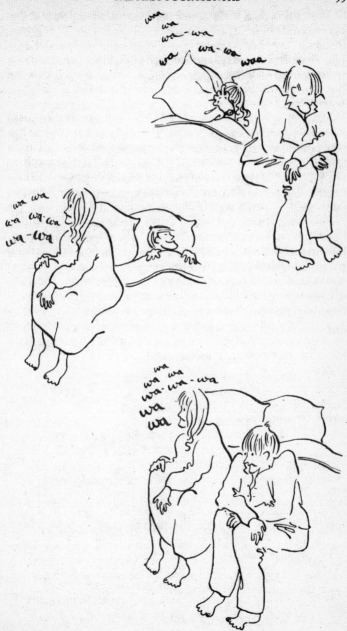

Once the baby is sucking well, if he is wide awake throughout the feed and obliges by filling his nappy while you are feeding him, instead of just after you have changed him — and always change him after a feed — you may get through a feed in about half to three-quarters of an hour. But certainly, during the first few weeks when both you and the baby are unaccustomed to this new experience, you can figure on at least an hour or more for each feed.

Now multiply that by five or six feeds — most babies start with six feeds a day if they are breast-feeding. Six hours out of your day, if all pushed together, would be most of a working day, say from 9.00 to 1.00 and from 2.00 to 4.00. Even spaced out, as it will be, six hours out of your waking day and part of your night, is a lot of time for feeding. Add three hours for preparing and eating your own meals — and you shouldn't be spending *any* time on preparation other than cooking — and you already have a nine hour day. Throw in another half hour, when you get adept at it, for the baby's bath, a half hour for your own bath (to help the vaginal region to heal), and at least another half hour for doing the baby's laundry. Even emptying the nappy bucket, tossing the nappies into the washing machine and hanging them up all takes time, plus the hand washing of delicate woollens and nylon or plastic pants. If you have a twin tub or are using the sterilization method — rinsing nappies out by hand — it will take longer. Your existence might begin to look something like this:

2.00- 3.00 am	Feed, wind and change	
3.00- 6.00 am	Sleep	
6.00- 7.00 am	Feed, wind and change	
7.00- 8.30 am	Dressing and your own breakfast	I found this a good time for a lie-in, until about 9.30. It does, however, mean that you miss seeing your husband at breakfast.
8.30- 9.00 am	Baby's bath	
9.00-10.00 am	Nappy washing, tidying house	
10.00-11.00 am	Feed, wind and change	
11.00- 1.00 am	Nap (later shopping or visits)	
1.00- 2.00 pm	Your own lunch	
2.00- 3.00 pm	Feed, wind and change	
3.00- 5.00 pm	Nap (after shopping or visits, or nappy washing if it is more convenient to dry nappies inside your living area overnight)	
5.00- 6.00 pm	Minimum meal preparation (the baby is	

almost invariably awake; or baby's bath if your husband gets home early enough to share it or to take turns giving the baby a bath)

6.00- 7.00 pm	Feed, wind and change
7.00- 8.30 pm	Your own meal
8.30-10.00 pm	Your own bath, shampoo, time to relax with husband (or sleep if you haven't managed a nap or two)
10.00-11.00 pm	Feed, wind and change
11.00- 2.00 am	Sleep

Laid out like this, it may look like you have several oases of time, from 11.00-1.00 (two hours) and from 3.00-5.00 (2 hours), a total of four hours. But remember that you will need to catch up a minimum of three hours of sleep. Theoretically, that leaves you with only an hour for shopping or visits, reading the newspaper or 'unscheduled' cuddling and playing with the baby once he starts to stay awake. If you happen to have a baby who likes to be awake and crying from the very beginning, well, you can see what happens to this lovely plan — it goes straight out the window!

Most babies tend to give up the sixth feed after a few weeks, unless you happen to be blessed with a hefty, hungry monster as my second child was, who kept to his six feeds, thank you, until solid food passed his lips at four months.

With a bit of luck, your baby might give up at least one of the night feeds before, maybe even both if the last night feed is sufficiently late, say at eleven o'clock at night, and the first one in the morning is sufficiently early, perhaps at five o'clock. The trouble is, the feeds depend upon when *he* decides they will be. Unfortunately, you can't make him eat when he's not ready. You may groan at the prospect of an eleven o'clock and a five o'clock feed, but this would give you an uninterrupted five hours of blessed slumber. Such are the small luxuries of motherhood!

Mobility

Before having a baby, I remember deciding that I was not going to suffer from the loneliness or isolation that so many mothers of young children are said to experience. I was going to load the baby into the pram or pushchair and march out into the world, summer or winter, to drop in on friends, or to take drives to nearby beauty spots that I had always meant to visit but never had the time for when I was working.

Oh yes, I had it all planned. Staying at home and looking after the baby would mean freedom, I thought. No more constraints of working hours, and busy evenings catching up on domestic chores like washing and ironing. No, I would zip through the housework, and the baby and I would rush out and enjoy life.

The reality went more like this. During those first few weeks after the birth of our first baby (and the second), I was so doggedly tired that it was all I could manage to keep going through the day and night feeds with feeding of adults and nappy washing (even with a washing machine) and the occasional nap in between.

After those first six weeks, when our first baby gave up night feeds (lucky us), I began to recover my strength, but it still seemed much easier to wait for my husband to heave the carrycot in and out of the car on Saturdays for the weekly shopping trip, not to mention carrying the groceries.

Looking back, I have to admit that it must have been easily eight or ten weeks after the baby's birth before I ventured out for one of my long promised walks. Well, it *was* a particularly cold, snowy winter that year, and I didn't want to risk a tiny newborn baby catching cold, I told myself. The real reason was that it was such an enormous physical effort, and feeds were so unpredictable (so were bowel movements) that timing was all important.

Eventually, I began to get the hang of it. For best results, I would set out immediately after feeding and changing the baby, thereby giving myself the maximum time before she would start crying for the next feed.

Even with a car, shopping was a bit of a performance. First, the baby would be dressed in her going-out gear, tucked into the carrycot and wheeled to the garage. I would then set the brake on the pram, get the car out of the garage, lift the carrycot into the back seat and strap it in (otherwise the carrycot and its contents might fly up or slide off the back seat with a quick stop), fold up the collapsible wheels and put them in the boot, and stash the bags — my handbag, the nappy bag (with a drink of fruit juice just in case), and the shopping basket — into the car.

If I were fortunate enough to find a parking place near the shops, the same procedure would take place twice in town: unpacking the wheels, installing the carrycot on the wheels, and again, loading them all back into the car after the shopping, and once again, at home. If there was much shopping, too much to fit into the shopping tray of the pram wheels (an absolute essential if you haven't a car) or the bags were too heavy to hang from the pram handle clips (available from the chemist), I would make two or three trips back and forth from the shops to the car with the groceries — hence, the need for a parking place close to the shops. So shopping takes longer.

As it happens, there is a weekly market in our town, but it only took a couple of teeth-gritting weeks to give that up. Wielding a pram through leisurely shopping crowds where knots of people stop to chat in the narrow passages between stalls (you are stuck as irretrievably as behind a lorry in a traffic jam, except that you're pushing the lorry), was not my idea of fun. So through trial and error, I quickly discovered the least popular times for shopping, when the shops were empty, and made it a point of going then. Not only did it keep me from cursing the local populace, but it enabled me to get through the shops faster and, therefore, with less risk of the baby getting hungry (and crying) before I got home.

On the few occasions when the baby wanted a feed while we were out shopping, it was back to the car for a feed, which can be fairly easily accomplished, even a breast-feed, with coat open and jumper pulled up, and the baby tucked warmly inside, passers-by none the wiser.

Had I not had a car to retreat to, there would have been *nowhere* in our small town to go to give the baby a feed. Perhaps there is in yours? I would either have had to put up with the crying and hard-heartedly continue the shopping with everyone glaring at the horrible mother, or abandon the shopping and head for home, the crying wafting onto the winter air for the duration of the walk. Sometimes a drink of fruit juice or water, or a dummy, will hold off the wailing for a time, but not always. If you live a very long walk from the shops, this cuts into your actual shopping time, so you will either have to make several short shopping trips or, much easier, wait until there is an available car.

Apart from the critical timing of your shopping expeditions, there is the difficulty of manoeuvering a pram in and out of shops, and above ground level. In my own small market town there are numerous shops that have one or two steps to get up to the door. Coping with one step is easy; you get the front wheels up, hold onto the pram, standing beside it, and unlatch the door, using the pram as a gentle ram to push it the rest of the way open. With two steps, unless they are extraordinarily wide, it is impossible to hold the door open at the same time as you are heaving both sets of wheels up a step. Usually, in a small shop, an assistant will notice your plight and come to your aid — or another mother. It is almost invariably a woman, who remembers what it was like wielding a pram, who comes to your rescue — but sometimes a father will hitch one end of the pram up the steps.

In the larger town near where I live, the department stores have lifts. In one, the lifts may only be operated by a member of staff, so first you have to find an assistant who isn't busy. Where there are only escalators, it is tricky. But a pram can be manoeuvered by rolling the front wheels on and then holding the wheels nearest you in the air for the duration of the ascent; or you can achieve the same result in reverse by stepping onto the escalator resting the rear wheels behind you (facing down) with the pram's front wheels suspended in the air until you reach the top.

Having said all this about prams, you can actually avoid buying a pram or carrycot altogether if you have no car and take the pushchair everywhere you go, letting the baby sleep in a cot at home. It used to be the case that babies had to stay in carrycots or prams until they could sit up — and they still shouldn't be made to sit up in a pushchair until they are able to sit up independently. But, recently, pushchairs have been manufactured that can accommodate even a newborn baby, as the back lays back almost flat so that the baby can sleep, with a sunshade to keep the light out of his eyes. Whether you buy the new drop-back version or, eventually after the baby is sitting up, the old stationary-back style pushchair, it should above all be light, which makes life infinitely more mobile and easier. There is no point in replacing a pram with another equally heavy contraption.

Another solution to the bulky pram problem is to carry the baby in a pouch on your chest or back. This has the advantage of leaving your hands free for the shopping and pushing a trolley, which will hold considerably more than a hand basket. You can't push both a pram or pushchair *and* a shopping trolley! And it isn't wise to leave a baby in a pram or pushchair unguarded these days.

I used an easy rider carrying pouch a few times, but the baby gained weight so quickly that it wasn't long before the combined weight of the baby and the groceries became too heavy. Maybe you have a stronger back or are used to back-packing? The disadvantage to the carrying pouch is that it can be awkward to get it onto your back with the baby in it, unaided. To carry it on the chest is easier, but not very comfortable if you have heavy, milk-swollen breasts underneath.

Still, while you are at the pram stage, it is possible to fulfil those lovely images in the baby catalogues of the happy mum and dad pushing the pram across the meadows. In fact, a walk with the pram is the easiest possible family outing — over reasonably smooth terrain. Forget rambler trails unless you use a carrying pouch or a metal-framed baby carrier on your back. Other easy outings are a ride in the car as you can stop whenever the baby needs a feed or changing, and visits to friends and relatives.

If you plot the feed times just right, you might park the pram beside your table and have a drink or a quick lunch in the garden of your favourite pub, but only in fine, reasonably warm weather. Should the baby wake up and cry, your drink or lunch will probably be cut short as you leave to avoid annoying other patrons. Gone are the days when you can chat with the regulars at the bar inside. Theoretically, babies under two are allowed in pubs (presumably as long as they can be held) provided it is in a separate room away from the bar, but I have even been asked to remove a pram from a family room! In that particular pub children were allowed, but not babies! It is best to check with the publican before descending, perhaps to be turned away.

Another easy outing is an evening out at the home of friends, taking the baby cosily tucked up in the carrycot to snooze in another room until he needs a feed — provided you can stay awake yourself!

Breaking Away

Mothers can never clock off, or rather, the only off-duty is spelled *out and away*. Because a mother will probably spend a lot more time with the baby than her husband, it is *her* ears that become finely tuned to hear the tiniest squeak or wheeze, and it is this constant listening that builds up tension on days when she may think that she hasn't actually done very much, and which leave her feeling worn out at the end of the day.

As we have already discussed earlier, it is a good idea for a new mother and her husband to start going out alone sometimes, even for very short breaks — for a drink, an evening class, a quick meal, to see friends — even while the baby is quite young. Nobody has ever pinned down exactly when young babies begin to become aware of strangers, so it is just as well to let your baby become accustomed to someone, who might become a regular babysitter, so that they will never be a stranger, but someone the baby will have known from the beginning.

This time together is important for you and your husband just now. I am not being overly dramatic when I say that a couple with a new baby has become a triangle. Though you may adore your husband, inevitably your baby's needs will have pushed those of your husband into second place; and besides having to meet a lot of new demands on his own time and energy as a father, he will have suddenly lost a large slice of your concentrated companionship.

Sex

Doubtless your GP will have advised you to try love-making at least once before the six weeks post natal check-up, to see if it is painful. If you happen to be one of the 24 per cent of women who have an episiotomy, or even if you only have tears, sex may be painful to you for some months after the birth. More likely you will feel so tired that sex will be the last thing on your mind. All you will probably want is sleep, sleep, and more sleep — until the baby gives up the night feeds.

If you have what is termed a 'normal' birth, with no stitches and no tears, you may only feel sore for a few days. Sheila Kitzinger, one of the founders of The National Childbirth Trust, and a noted authority in antenatal education, made a study into the effects of stitches, tears and episiotomies, from which I quote below:

> A woman who has had a normal labour is usually quite ready physiologically for intercourse a week or ten days after delivery. But she may feel rather guilty that her preoccupation with the baby, as she lies listening for its cries or worrying whether it is breathing, makes her less enthusiastic than her partner. He knows he must be gentle, but is often given little or no instruction as to how he can be. Tenderness can be inadequate, because if he is vacillating or nervous the attempt can prove unsatisfying for both.
>
> The natural lubrication which is secreted by means of a deep vasocongestive reaction to stimulation in the tissues around the vaginal barrel often does not return for several weeks. It is therefore wise to have some sort of lubrication before penetration, and this can be introduced by the man himself with a stroking movement.
>
> An effect of many popular books on sex is that a man encountering a negative response to his advances in his mate tends to concentrate attention entirely upon an organ which he has learned is of superordinate importance for her sexual arousal — the clitoris. He attempts clitoral stimulation, often heavy-handedly for far too long.
>
> This is of particular relevance after childbirth, when a man may be apprehensive about touching the vagina itself in case he should cause the woman pain. The most effective technique is then, not concentration of stimulation of the clitoris, but light touch on the other parts of the body, and stroking of the abdomen, breasts, back and thighs. Probably any part of a woman's body can become an erogenous zone *if it is touched in the right way*.
>
> With the first acts of intercourse after childbirth, even though a lubricant cream or jelly is used, the scar area may itself give rise to pain. Pressure of the penis should then be directed forwards, towards the clitoris, rather than down towards mucocutaneous

juncture of the vaginal mucosa and the perineum. This can most easily be effected by variation in coital posture and with the help of pillows.

The ventro-ventral position in which the man is lying superior to the woman is likely to be a very bad posture from this point of view. Preferable variations are those in which the woman is kneeling astride the male partner and leaning *forwards*, not back, or in which the male partner lies *behind* her. In both positions the woman has freedom of movement, so that she can more easily assume an attitude in which she can avoid undue friction against the tender tissues and can achieve maximum stimulation.

Any position in which the male partner kneels or lies behind her also has the advantage of allowing her to grip the penis by contraction of gluteal muscles, so that she can further control the timing, and also the angle of penetration. She can excite and satisfy him with a combination of gluteal contractions and pelvis rocking, even though the shaft of the penis has not penetrated the vagina, while he gently stimulates the shaft of her clitoris. Many couples find that such a technique helps a process in which gradually, over a series of separate acts of intercourse, full penetration is effected, and orgasm and fulfilment experienced by both partners. (*Episiotomy: Physical and Emotional Aspects*, edited by Sheila Kitzinger, published by The National Childbirth Trust.)

The simple message is: if and when you get around to sex between the feeds and the naps, take it easy if it hurts, use a lubricant, and try one of the positions that you enjoyed during the last months of pregnancy to take the strain off your tender regions. Don't expect flashing lights straight away, but have faith that the shooting stars will return.

Mrs Kitzinger's study, quoted above, showed that many more women had much more pain, a lot longer after childbirth than anyone had before believed. If you happen to be one of the 22 per cent who suffer pain during intercourse for longer than three months after the birth of your baby, don't think that it's all in your head. Just follow Sheila Kitzinger's good advice, mention it to your GP, and wait. Tissues do heal with time.

Most women are so burdened by exhaustion during the first few months of their babies' lives that there is no question of boredom — just the determination to survive. It is after the baby starts solid food and begins to miss out the night feeds, one by one, that a new era begins to dawn. So chin up, there's a lull before the onslaught of crawling.

12. From Solid Food to Crawling

Life can suddenly begin to look rosy again whenever your baby starts to leave off the night feeds. To sleep undisturbed once again through an entire blissful night can be as sharp a relief as a cool drink of water at the end of a marathon to a new mother who has been dragging through the days and nights for several months. Not that your baby will necessarily oblige by sleeping through the night, every night, from the moment you start to give him solid food, but at least you can begin to hope that it will happen soon, once you do.

Solid Food

Hopefully you will have a hungry baby, who is willing to try anything that approaches his mouth, as my second child was. The first, bless her, brought out her mother's temper and first cross words at only four months old, when she resolutely refused even to open her mouth to try anything that appeared on a spoon.

What to do? I used to sit with my own mouth gaping open like a fool, repeating 'open wide' until I was hoarse; I used to nibble her baby food from her spoon, muttering, 'Um-um-um'. I strongly suspect that she knew exactly what I wanted her to do, but simply refused on the grounds that anything I asked her to do was not going to be particularly pleasant — like her bath.

In the end I started smearing her food on the outside of her mouth, curiosity got the better of her and she tasted it. Not that the battle was won. Oh no! What she tasted, she didn't like — cough, spew, all over mummy! So we went from one packet of baby cereal to another. In desperation, having consulted every other mother I knew, I finally found that the dehydrated vegetables — mixed green vegetables, carrots and tomatoes, and stage one baby food tomatoes and cheese — went in remarkably better than the cereals. To this day, we have to cajole her to eat her cereal in the morning!

One mum I know swears by a baby food grinder she bought at the chemist which will purée any food — meat, veg, or fruit combinations — to acceptable baby texture. She has found it easy to carry around and has even puréed food for her baby in restaurants, and only uses commercial baby foods when she and her husband are having curry.

As the time when a baby is starting to eat solid food usually coincides with a slackening off of the night feeds, a mother's motivation to get the baby eating is high. It doesn't take much, according to the baby books, only two or three spoonfuls, 'to get the baby used to different tastes'. I say, if you have a reluctant eater, stick to one new taste a week to keep the dramas to a minimum, and also so that the baby doesn't begin to associate mealtimes with a battle of wills.

From the end of the night feeds until your baby starts to crawl can be a fairly settled, even a relatively quiet time, with a bit of luck and a reasonably placid baby. Besides catching up on sleep, with fewer feeds, down to three or four a day, at last you have more time to do things that you have had to let go. Also, you should be able to predict more reliably when the baby will want his feeds, which means that you can plan a few expeditions with a freer mind.

By now, the baby will probably stay awake longer, will begin to take real notice of toys and his surroundings, and he will respond more to you, which makes him more fun to have around. Most babies are delighted to be propped up in a bouncing chair in the same room as you are so that they can watch you while you get on with whatever you are doing. In fact, you will find that he won't like it if you pop *out* of the room, even for a minute, leaving him alone — this is the beginning of the child's possessiveness of your company that rarely abates until he is at least three and settled in a nursery school or playgroup. You're his mum and he wants to be near you — heart-warming, flattering little creatures, babies!

Weaning

Just as you are beginning to recover your strength, get back into the habit of sex, hopefully, to get the baby weaned off the breast and settled into something like a predictable schedule, you may start thinking that life is rather dull. Especially if you have been too tired up to then, too hard-up to hire a babysiter, or the baby has been too unpredictable, for you to be able to go out happily, you may be wondering if life with a baby is really very much fun? Or put another way, will life ever get back to normal — pre-baby?

The answer, sadly, is NO. *Once you have a baby, life will never, ever be anything like it was before.* When a child arrives, gone are those glorious carefree evenings when you and your husband could suddenly decide to pop out for a drink at the pub (unless it's warm and the pub has a garden). Gone are those spontaneous, romantic walks into the sunset. Now, it's a project to arrange a babysitter; and as it becomes a project, it usually goes by the board. By the time it's arranged, the sunset has vanished. During the day, so much has to be packed in case it is needed for the baby, and the timing of every outing plotted around the baby's feeding and sleeping requirements that you can easily fall into the lazy habit of asking yourself, is it worth the trouble? (Emphatically, yes!) Even at the end of the day when all you want is to put your feet up and yawn at the television set, you have to remain alert, on duty, with an ear cocked for the baby's cry. Should you decide to keep your job, to hire a live-in nanny, and even if you have a house-keeper as well, you will still be a mother and have to — and want to — respond to the needs of your baby when you are at home.

But once the baby is weaned is the time when you can at last feel free of that invisible umbilical cord from baby to breast. Ironically, often this is when new mothers start to feel how much they are missing the chat they used to enjoy at the office, miss their friends, and feel left out of what everyone else is doing. I say ironically because the first long siege is over, the euphoria and the worst tiredness of the first few weeks and months has passed, and hey presto — boredom sets in.

It is often just at this point of first freedom from the tyranny of the feeding schedule that mothers feel most tied down. Although they may have long looked forward to reaching this goal, upon reaching it they suddenly realize that babies go on being a tremendous tie. Their needs for feeds and naps must be respected or you pay the consequences — a tired, bellowing or whining baby.

I admire enormously those intrepid souls who will go to any length to carry on their own adult pursuits with the baby in pram or backpack, but unless you can count yourself among them — and can manage to feel carefree despite a wailing, tired and bored baby — then you must forget skiing, deep sea diving, sailing, or long-distance walking, unless you hire a babysitter, or until your baby or youngest child is at least four or older. You will find that these sports are too dangerous, and either mum gets lumbered looking after the baby while dad goes off, or both parents have to take turns child-minding and, therefore, are unable to share the fun. If you drag the little one along, he will be so miserable — in musuems, for example — that you may have to leave and may as well not have come.

It is not until a child reaches the age when he can go to school (or nursery school or playgroup) that a mother can once again enjoy walking briskly through the high street unhampered by a pram, pushchair, reins, or a small hand dragging her behind, unless the father, granny, or a babysitter, stays at home with the child.

How to beat the boredom? Well, enjoy the lull until your baby starts to crawl. If there is a long string of novels that you have always wanted to read, if there is sewing or knitting — perhaps a new outfit for you or the baby — that you have been meaning to start, or experimenting with new recipes (making sure that there is ample preparation time between feeds), this is the time for such pursuits. Invite friends around as often as possible, and take the baby for walks. Once having weaned the baby, if you are still a bit chubby around the middle or bottom, this is the time to get trim. It will give you a tremendous lift, and an excuse maybe for some new clothes, or a holiday?

Sitting Up

Once a baby can sit up, you will need to move him out of the carrycot in the car, which is no longer safe, and into a child's safety carseat. You may still be able to use the carrycot for taking the baby anywhere where you want to stay long enough for him to sleep (if he still fits) — once you've arived. Be careful over the type of carseat you choose. Countless times I have been grateful for having bought the sort that has a foam-backed cover (warm in winter) that can be whipped off and all the crumbs, spilt orange juice and milk washed out, and quickly dried overnight.

Once in a carseat, most babies will only tolerate going short distances, an hour or an hour-and-a-half (although some will sleep peacefully in their seats) before they want to stop and romp around, and then they usually don't want to get back into their carseats!

At home, if you haven't already, the baby should be moved into a cot as he may try to climb out of the carrycot, or tip it over.

Mobility

In addition to the outings suggested earlier with younger babies, I found with the aid of a carrying pouch, and either my husband or another mum to help me to get the baby into it, once arrived at our destination, that the period from about four to six months, (after which the baby became too heavy) was a good time to visit museums and National Trust properties and gardens. Getting a pram up steps to a museum, and usually there are a lot of steps in National Trust properties, is difficult. So a carrying pouch solves the problem.

I used to go on such outings with another mother and we soon devised a good 'schedule': we would drive in two cars (in order to strap both carrycots safely in) to the museum or stately home; feed the babies in our cars and have a picnic snack ourselves; and then would strap the dozy babies into their pouches for our stroll around. With experience, we even got confident enough to take the prams into the National Trust restaurants for lunch if it wasn't too crowded — after feeding the babies.

Some stately homes will allow you to take prams or pushchairs through, but you need to check in advance. By the time a baby has reached the pushchair stage, he may find being pushed through an elegant old house rather boring. But it depends upon the child: our daughter enjoyed it; our son was bored stiff and kept trying to climb out of the pushchair.

Depending upon how quickly you regain your energy, this might be a good time to return the invitations of friends who invited you to dinner during the baby's first few months. But don't go mad; there is no need to prove that you're a five-star chef just yet. Plan something easy; make dishes that can be easily held so that if the baby wakes up at just the wrong moment, the next course won't be spoiled. You can save the soufflé for next year.

If you haven't done so before now, this is certainly the time to introduce your baby to a babysitter. As I have said before, babies couldn't care less who looks after them during their first few months, but sometime, usually when they are between six and eight months old, they suddenly become selective. So let your baby get to know as many would-be babysitters as possible before he reaches the age of discrimination. Otherwise, you may end up like of friend of mine who virtually never went out in the evening with her husband for the first two years of her child's life for fear that the baby might wake up and be frightened at not finding mummy there!

Now that the baby is having fewer and more predictable feeds, you can arrange longer escapes for yourselves — a disco, the theatre, a concert, dinner with friends — but you will still be tied by that feeding schedule if you are breast-feeding. This will generally last until the baby is between six and seven months old, although some mothers valiantly carry on breast-feeding until their infants are a year old — if the child is unwilling to give up breastfeeding, even up to two!

This is also a good time to explore any mother-and-baby groups in your neighbourhood. (Ask at the Citizen's Advice Bureau, the Library, the Town Hall, at any of the churches, or the local group of the National Childbirth Trust. Take along a blanket, a large towel, or a babynest to lay your baby on so that he can watch from floor level and become acquainted with the other tinies before they all start crawling and toddling. (He won't see much from a pram.)

Another tip — if you plan to use a playpen, this is the time to get the baby accustomed to it, either lying on his back, waving his arms and legs in the air, or lying on his tummy so that he can watch you. There are various arguments for and against playpens.

For: you can pop the baby in and race to the telephone, the door, or rush out to bring in the laundry if it starts to rain, with a reasonable degree of certainty that the baby will come to no harm. If the baby is used to being in the playpen before he is mobile, you *may* be able to have short breaks later on when you know that the baby is safe without watching his every move.

Against: babies, as soon as they are mobile, are in the business of discovering the world, and learning about it through their investigations. If you limit the baby's field of play to a small area with an assortment of toys with which he fairly quickly becomes familiar — and so bored — you are not allowing your child the freedom to develop and learn as quickly as he might. Also, the baby will very possibly reject the playpen, whether or not you get him used to it, the moment he becomes mobile, screaming the house down whenever you put him in it, and you will have spent money on a fairly expensive bit of equipment — unless you wisely bought the playpen second-hand or borrowed it.

For what it's worth, most of the mothers I know have found that the open-sided wooden playpens are less apt to be rejected than the round mesh-sided ones, from which the baby can't see you so well.

During this lull while your baby stays put is not the time to think, 'Well, I seem to have everything pretty well under control . . . perhaps we should start another baby.' Not, at least, until you have read the next chapter.

I know some women who think it would be marvellous to have two babies as close together as possible, in order to get the nappies over with all at once and to shorten the length of time before both children go to school. Certainly, they have a point, but I consider them to be very brave souls, for the next few months when a baby starts to crawl can be very difficult and to my mind it is better not to face them in the throes of pregnancy. But read on, it's your decision.

13. Another Baby Now?

There is no particular 'ideal' age gap between children. But a very random sampling of the mothers I know, who are in the midst of rearing very young children, does throw some light on the problems and advantages of various age gaps.

Obviously, the closer together you have your babies, the shorter the period of intensive maternal servitude, but *intensive* is the operative word. Still, how fortunate we are these days even to be able to debate the subject — after all, our own mothers were pretty much lumped with a new baby whenever it came!

Close Together — Up to An Eighteen-Month Gap

When your first baby is six months old, having got through the night feeds and with the baby settled into a fairly civilized pattern of four feeds and two naps a day, you might think that looking after a new baby as well wouldn't be too strenuous. Well, if you could snap your fingers and have the new baby appear, you might be right. But add nine months to your first baby's six months, and your first baby would be fifteen months old when the second was born. At anytime from eight to twelve months old, usually, he would have started to crawl, just when you would be probably feeling tired from the pregnancy; and by the time the baby was born, your firstborn at fifteen months old would probably still be at the precarious first stages of walking.

Through both the crawling and early walking stages, a mother must give constant attention to the toddler during his every waking moment to keep him out of harm; and when he is walking, picking him up and soothing him when he keeps falling over, bruising his dignity if not bumping his head and grazing his knees. To my way of thinking, this terribly demanding time is not the best moment to have a baby.

Suppose you start another baby when your first is nine to ten months old, making your first born eighteen or nineteen months old when the second appears? Nineteen months is a slightly easier age, in that by the time the second baby arrives the older child might be more sure on his feet. He *might* or might not be just at the brink of potty-training when the new baby appears on the scene. But feeling insecure with the arrival of a new brother or sister, he will almost certainly revert to baby-like behaviour, which baby books, doctors and health visitors call *regression*, an attempt to recapture your attention and affection. His subconscious thinking is: 'I got all of mummy's attention and love when I was a baby. Here's this *other* baby getting mummy's attention. If I act like him, like a baby again, I'll get mummy's attention back!'

It matters not a whit when you potty-train either child as long as you manage it before they go to school; although it is convenient to have done it by the time they are three, before they go to nursery school or playgroup. But having an older child in nappies does mean that you have nappies for *two* to do every day! In our climate, a drier could cease to look like a luxury and begin to look like a necessity unless you are fortunate enough to have a large, guaranteed warm, indoor drying area. And besides the nappies, remember, there is still the household linen, your own, and your husband's clothes to keep laundered.

Having babies very close together also has social implications. Just when a woman is beginning to catch her breath, and to regain some of her energy after the onslaught of night feeds and lost sleep — and the social isolation that almost inevitably accompanies the night-feed era — that social isolation starts all over again with the birth of her second baby, and it often lasts more or less until she finishes the second period of night feeds.

Having a relatively young older child carries the advantage that she *might* be able to cat nap during his naps; but if she finds it difficult to drop off at precisely the times of her older child's naps, the period of recuperation will take longer after the second baby than the first, as she has less chance to catch up on sleep during the day. The result (and I remember it well) is that poor mother is so tired by the time she gets the supper on the table that she can hardly eat it for wanting to drop into bed immediately afterwards. As this goes on evening after evening her relationship with her husband diminishes, almost to nonexistence. He sees her over the supper table, and possibly at breakfast during the week, and only a little more at weekends as she grabs the chance of afternoon naps on Saturday and Sunday.

To say that she is too tired for a social life outside the family is an understatement. Only with great determination can a woman make the effort to go out for short breaks with her husband, a drive with the family in the back seat, an hour's shopping, or a quick meal out. It is so much easier just to slump in front of the television set and let it lull her to sleep.

However, undoubtedly there are advantages to having two babies close together: a shorter period of nappies; a shorter period of intensive baby-minding; a shorter time off work altogether if you have decided to wait to return until the youngest child goes to school; the two children are more likely to be company for one another if they don't fight tooth and nail (unpredictable); and you may get by with only one set of toys at a time, though you might actually have to have more toys to avoid too much friction.

Twins or More

Seeing twins always brings a smile to people's faces. The only thing more charming than one baby is two. But one stalwart mother of twins I know put it like this: 'From the moment they were born, I never had an instant to myself until they reached the age of two!'

Twins are born competitive, for their mother's time, attention, and affection, and more basically, for their very feeds. Inevitably, one baby yells louder and longer, and possibly later, hits harder, pulls hair and pinches unmercifully. A mother is pulled in two directions, tries desperately to be fair and frequently feels guilty that she never quite is.

Stating the obvious, there are twice as many nappies, clothes and bedclothes to wash, twice as many formulas to prepare (if you bottle feed). It will take much longer to feed two, simply because of the difficulty of getting both babies comfortable simultaneously and feeding together, which means more sleep lost. Just when you think you have both comfortable and feeding, one falls asleep, gets wind or needs changing. Multiply the dressing and undressing, changing, feeding and bathing by two, and you begin to see the magnitude of the double-duty on our flimsy timetable.

This is to say nothing of the double expense: a double carrycot, a bigger (estate) car to accommodate it, a double drop-back pushchair, two sets of clothes, twice the number of nappies, blankets and sheets; and later on, times two the cost of piano lessons, cub scout uniforms, etc., you can tot up the rest. At least with children of different ages, it is odds on that the expenses don't always fall at exactly the same time.

An Eighteen-Month to Two-and-a-half-Year Gap

With a slightly wider gap, you have a fighting chance that the older child will have conquered walking, might have passed the stage of potty-training, and be sufficiently comprehending that you can explain all about the arrival of the new baby and engage his help with small tasks to make him feel very much needed: 'Please bring me a clean nappy,' 'Could you open the drawer and hand me the baby's blue sweater?' Small requests that he can fulfil make the older child feel very valued at a time when he is feeling displaced.

Once the new baby starts to sit up, the older child can begin to play with him, and once walking, they are playmates; though the older child's activities have to be somewhat restricted so that small dangerous objects are kept out of the grasp and gullet of the baby.

The older child, however, might have given up naps altogether which, as I have mentioned before, means that it will take a mother longer to recuperate than if she were able to drop into bed when the firstborn had naps. This leads to the predictable loss of social life and isolation which, I suspect, happens whenever a new baby is born, no matter what the age gap, during the period of night feeds. But having had a lull of a year or so between the periods of night feeds, she will, hopefully, have had the opportunity to revive her social life before the second onslaught.

An older child is still apt to suffer regression. If he has been successfully potty-trained, with the arrival of the new baby, he is likely to start having accidents for a time. He may copy baby noises, which can be unnervingly distressing to a mother at a time when she is trying to encourage him to widen his vocabulary. He will demand that his requests be met immediately or resort to screaming, crying and kicking. All this when his mother most needs his co-operation because she is overly tired and, as a result, probably lacking in patience.

This slightly wider age gap can also make travelling difficult. The two children have different needs for sleep, go to bed at different times, and therefore, unless they are accustomed to sharing a room at home, will keep one another awake away on weekend visits or on holidays. A few nights of the adjustment of two children sleeping in one room — waking each other during the night, and bright-eyed chirpy children at 5.00 a.m. — can leave parents so exhausted that they wish they'd never gone away. There are other solutions, like getting the children used to sharing a room at home before the holiday, or keeping one child, usually the younger, in the parents' room; but you run the risk of the child sleeping alone feeling rejected. Yet another solution is for the parents to split up and each have a child in his or her room; but this isn't much fun for the parents.

A two-and-a-half to three-and-a-half year difference is probably the most popular age gap, so we will discuss this in detail later (Chapter 18).

14. Crawling to Walking

Most parents are eager for their offspring to start to crawl. I remember my husband anxiously trying to teach our baby daughter to move forwards instead of backwards. When she finally got it, life became hell.

A crawling baby is a tiny potential calamity, drawn to danger like a pin to a magnet. A crawler's imagination for finding ways to injure, if not kill himself, seems to be infinite. It isn't that I live in a particularly dangerous or difficult house. Let me say here — no house can be completely childproof. You can merely do your best:

— install safety catches on *every* low cupboard;
— install out-of-reach hooks (or locks, but then, you have to keep track of the keys) on any doors to cupboards or rooms that you don't want the baby to go into (the boiler room, for instance);
— put safety covers over low electrical outlets;
— remove any easily toppled furniture such as nests of tables and standard lamps;
— remove all plants and breakable or delicate ornaments such as ashtrays and vases, from any reachable furniture that might be pushed over;
— install stairguards at the top and bottom of the stairs;
— get a large mesh fireguard for the fireplace;
— find substitutes for any free-standing gas, electric or paraffin fires that might be pushed over or burn the baby if touched;
— and move all weed killers, cleansers, soaps, disinfectants, poisons or medicines to very high, or preferably locked cupboards (soon enough your baby will learn to climb).

It's a wonder that babies — or their parents — live through the crawling era, but somehow most do. It is a case of your wits against the baby's, and only natural that he should eagerly apply all of his senses — to look, listen, touch, smell, and taste — to investigate his brave new world.

Even if you follow all of the suggestions above, I can almost guarantee that your baby will find that the logs or coal make excellent toys, if not edibles, that the loo paper is for pulling and pulling, that the loo is quite a fun place to play in, and that one day you will forget to push a cupboard door quite closed and the baby will discover all of its delightful contents. Or when you go to answer the telephone or the door, the baby will suddenly disappear into thin air — only to be found hiding beneath a piece of furniture or behind a curtain, giggling like a lunatic as you pull him out, half relieved and half angry!

From the moment your baby starts to crawl, and this usually coincides with his needing fewer naps, you must watch his every waking moment to keep him from harm or disaster! A mother must be constantly attentive, following the crawler, anticipating his next curiosity-driven calamity along his route to discovery.

Even in a huge, grassy, fenced-in garden, the baby will make straight for the stray bramble poking through the fence just at eye level. Outdoors offers a wide variety of misadventure: stones, sand and dirt to eat; worms and bugs to taste; flowers to pick, if not pull up; not to mention all of the tantalizing bright-coloured berries on bushes to pick and swallow.

Friends used to say, 'Why don't you put a lawn chair in the garden and just let the baby get on with it while you have a sunbathe?' I tried it, and was up and down out of the chair like a yo-yo — it was much easier just to stand in the centre of the garden, like a ringmaster, ready to run in any direction. With a crawler, a mother must never allow her concentration to wander. Pick up a newspaper or open a book, and if you can't see the baby out of the corner of your eye, it's time to go and see what he is up to. This is a period of concentrated child-minding which, no matter how relaxed a mother is in her attitudes, is very tiring. The tension is enormous.

Consider any job, even those that demand a lot of concentration. None that I can think of requires the constant vigilance, the tension from being instantly ready to jump and run with such high stakes — the baby's life. I can think of no other job that demands this kind of constant readiness, other than, perhaps, active military service!

It's during the crawling stage that those who have perhaps risked the expense and the possibility of the baby rejecting a playpen, but who nevertheless started getting the baby accustomed to it early on, reap the benefit. They can drop the baby into the playpen *en route* to the telephone or the door. They even have the luxury of going to the loo in private (otherwise the baby can find all sorts of mischief during those few minutes that you disappear).

I have often wished that I could somehow tether the baby outside in the centre of the lawn. Even with a baby harness, it is not safe to leave a baby strapped unseen in a highchair. He just might be able to make the highchair tip over. The only three places that you can legitimately tie the baby down, so to speak, are with a safety harness in his highchair, in his pushchair, or in a child's car seat.

Many are the times that I have seen a mother pushing a pram or a pushchair through driving rain, not solely out of the necessity to get to the shops I am certain, now that I am a mother, but out of the need to relax the constant vigilance at home. No matter how long the walk, it is much more relaxing to push the child in his pushchair than to stay at home, waiting, watching, and leaping to meet each new disaster.

To say that this is a tiring, tense-making, frustrating period is an understatement. By this time, most mothers have recovered their strength sufficiently that they are somewhat bored by being homebodies and would enjoy a bit of company. But it's best to choose your friends from among those who have children and understand the problems, and are willing to dismantle their houses in order to accommodate you and your baby. A visit to childless friends with knick-knack laden coffee tables can be such a tension-packed performance that it defeats the purpose as you leap to prevent the baby from pulling down the plants, yanking over the lamps by their cords, and toppling the smaller pieces of furniture.

The only reasonably easy social gathering that you and the baby can go to during this period are mother-and-baby, or mother-and-toddler, groups — held either in community halls or in other mothers' child-oriented homes. Don't expect much conversation. Other mothers will have to do the same yo-yo, leaping up and down to retrieve their babies, so conversation tends to be telegraphically brief, due to the inevitable interruptions. But at least you will find that other women are going through the same siege, and perhaps collect a telephone number or two to ring up while the baby is napping or after he goes to sleep at night. Misery does love company.

More than ever before, this is the time when you and your husband *must* get out alone together. Find a way, somehow.

To be sure, your husband can help in the surveillance at

weekends, but don't expect him to be able instantly to anticipate all of the dangers. You will have to warn him of what dangers the baby has already discovered, and ask him if he will watch (not while he cuts the grass or watches TV), but really watch the baby. Put more positively, you might suggest things that would interest the baby, or supply toys that the baby can do something with — pans and lids, large cardboard boxes to crawl into, plastic cups and a plastic bowl of water.

Depending upon the length of time that the baby naps, you may still have one, or even two, oases of times to yourself during the day — for ironing, cooking, sewing (too dangerous now with a crawler underfoot who might pull the iron cord, the sewing machine cord — pulling the machine down on top of him, or get hold of a pin cushion). Personally I tend to grasp these oases with both hands and sink into a chair for a cup of tea, my own lunch, for a quick read of the newspaper, or to make those necessary telephone calls.

It is pointless to expect a crawling baby to understand 'Yes' and 'No', or so the psychologists tell us. But neither do they tell us *when* babies start to understand individual words. My theory is to carry on as though the baby understands, saying, 'No-no! Stay out of the coal.' 'No, don't go near the fire, hot! Burn!'

I was astonished to find that our firstborn actually took notice and backed away from the fire when told to at ten months old! Our second, well, he was certainly walking before he started to take any notice whatsoever. We can but try.

Mobility

By the time your baby starts to crawl, he will doubtless have graduated from the pram to a pushchair, which makes wading through slow-moving shopping crowds easier, but limits the number of bags you can carry looped over each handle (fewer than the pram tray would hold) before the pushchair becomes unbalanced.

Most babies love going for drives, providing you can cover the distance in an hour (or until the baby falls asleep in his carseat) followed by a picnic. In fact, I found the crawling era endurable so long as I could take the baby wherever I was going in her pushchair, and if there was enough for her to watch so that she wasn't bored, and therefore, eager to escape the restraint. This worked, between naps and feeds, for clothes shopping, for a quick trip to the hairdresser (not long enough for a perm), for visits to the dentist, to the doctor, to the garden of the local pub. The pushchair cuts out buildings having a lot of stairs, unless you can heave the weight of the baby in the pushchair unaided: you can never count on assistance.

As I have already mentioned, this is the time for mother-and-baby groups, or getting to know other mothers with children of nearly the same age as yours so that you can exchange visits in one another's child-oriented houses. Once out of the carrycot, as most crawling babies are, you won't be able any longer to stash your sleeping baby in a friend's back bedroom. You will be stuck with getting a babysitter to stay while you go out, unless you have a *very* amiable baby who will go to sleep in a travel cot in strange surroundings at the home of friends, for example, and then who doesn't mind being woken up to go home again.

The crawling era, like the period when your baby is smaller, is a good time for entertaining at home, the baby happily asleep upstairs in his own bed, and you and your friends downstairs (have you thought of carry-out suppers at one anothers' houses?)

If you have a placid, 'obedient' baby, you might try going to the beach. I say obedient, because some babies actually will stop eating the sand if you ask them nicely not to. As for others . . . well, I found that after fifteen minutes of chase-and-retrieve with my crawling baby, the best solution was to lock her in her pushchair for the duration of the picnic — hence, placid. If she starts to scream, you may as well pack up, keep chasing, or wait until next year. . .

15. End of Year Assessment

Most women find that the changes motherhood brings to their lives are so monumental that after a year they hardly recognize themselves, and therein lies a problem — what psychologists call a 'crisis of identity'.

If you are reading this before getting pregnant, or when you are pregnant, just consider your current circumstances. It is likely that you have a job, are well groomed, reasonably well paid, receive at least some job satisfaction and, possibly, consider yourself financially independent. As a result, you enjoy a certain amount of status amongst your friends and relatives, and in the community and, though you may never have stopped to think about it, a measure of self-respect. You have a certain amount of spare time to follow your favourite leisure pursuits, be they disco dancing or bell ringing, and probably you manage to find at least some money to spend as you please.

At the end of the first year of motherhood, times usually have changed. A stay-at-home mother has a job, certainly, but she doesn't get paid, unless you consider the child benefit fair pay! She may enjoy looking after the baby, but babies are terribly loath to mutter, 'Thank you, Mummy for the feed,' or 'Thanks a lot, Mum, that was a terrific nappy you just put on me.' You get little appreciation or gratitude for being a mother. Everyone, including your husband unless he is a paragon, will merely take mothering for granted. But ask any mother, and though she may find it difficult to put into words, it's the little things that make it somehow worthwhile.

With my youngest, I remember how he used to love his bath, how he loved to kick, and once or twice, laughed aloud almost before he could smile. He adored cuddly toys — he would clutch a fluffy ball, shaking it to make the bell jingle, or stare intently at a tiny panda bear as he held it up in front of his face. I remember how he loved it when I sang: no matter how hard he was crying, he would always stop to listen. And he was so cuddly; somehow he would grasp my clothes or wrap his arm around my neck as I held him. The preciousness of these things are difficult to explain to someone who has never had a child.

But mothers do not enjoy much status. More often you hear, 'Anyone can do it.' The fact that not everyone can do it well is seldom mentioned. Nor is it even easy to give yourself the credit of being a good mother. Almost by definition, being a good mother is such a subjective feeling, that even when you've had a good day and have been doing your very best, drop one cross word and your 'job satisfaction' is shot to hell with guilt.

The Mummy-frump

As for grooming: since I've been writing this book, I've taken note of the mothers of young children pushing prams and pushchairs up my high street, and it's done my flagging ego no end of good to realize that I'm not the only mummy-frump walking around. Mothers of young children resort to almost a uniform of jeans or trousers, washable pullovers, socks, and low, comfortable shoes. High heels are a hazard with a baby underfoot and babies are a hazard to tights. Mine loves nothing better than to grab hold of a pinch of tights until they ladder.

Doubtless a contributory factor towards the trend to mummy-frumpiness is the sheer difficulty of keeping whatever you are wearing looking neat and tidy. Hold a baby on your lap for five minutes and your clothes look like they've never been pressed. Babies are very messy little people, seemingly determined to spew either milk or food over the front of whatever you're wearing, especially anything pale or white. If they miss at mealtimes, you can be sure they'll make up for it by grabbing at shiny earrings and brooches, or throttle you with your own necklace or scarf.

Most mothers of very young children, I've noticed, simply give up wearing any jewellery or scarves except rings and durable bangle bracelets during the day when their babies are around; being unaccessorized they don't look particularly well put together, but rather unchic, rumpled and frumpish. But although there may seem to be little point in putting on nice clothes if you are going to be at home all day where, unless you make a special effort to go out, you will see no other adult except your husband and the milkman from one day to the next, it is good for your ego to know that you are looking reasonably well. Yet during the early months, with little time between feeds, and when you have to prepare a nappy bag just to push the baby out to the shops, it's unlikely that you will risk cutting into your precious shopping time by stopping to change clothes.

We've already discussed the difficulty of getting to the hairdresser, but a regular trim will keep your confidence afloat better than letting your hair grow shaggy. For the same reason that there is little motivation to wear smart clothes — and heaven knows there is little time for putting on make-up or more than brushing your hair — many mothers keep putting off, and putting off, the diet to get their figures back. Enter the mummy-frump.

Physically, feeling knocked out every night, tense, and possibly still overweight, which adds up psychologically to feeling rather unattractive, can all contribute to a lowered desire for sex. 'Lowered?' A friend of mine chortled with a bitter laugh, 'There's a complete turn-off on sex!' It may not be as bad as that, but suffice it to say that you may be walking around in a state of slight depression. All of these little things merely add up to making you feel, as my friend put it, 'Not really myself for a year after the baby was born.'

You might not feel this way at all. You may have a three-hour labour, no episiotomy, no stitches and no tears; the baby may begin to sleep through the night before you go home from the maternity hospital; and you could find that you have immediately reverted to your normal weight. Lucky old you! But if you don't, it's perfectly normal and far more usual; so you needn't feel that you are different from anybody else. And most of us have lived through it!

As for money, now that you are no longer paid for your job, doubtless your joint income will have suffered, not to mention your financial independence. Where formerly you had some time for your own pastimes, with a baby you are at the beck and call of a tiny tyrant, who is totally selfish in his demands. Time for your own pleasures must be rigorously planned, and the money found for the babysitter. Result: fewer leisure activities.

Unless you have devoted friends, you will probably look back over the last year and find that you have seen much less of your childless and single friends. Let's hope that you will have started to make a few new friendships with other parents of young children so that you will be able to share the joy and, especially, the agonies.

It goes almost without saying that if you haven't already, this is the time for all good wives and mothers to pull themselves together, to shed the extra pounds, to make an effort, at least occasionally, to look smart (it is good for *your* morale), and to try to broaden the domestic scene to include a mother-and-baby or mother-and-toddler group, to join a babysitting circle, or to get a babysitter on a regular basis if at all possible (even if it's only once a month), so that you have something nice to look forward to — going out with your husband.

Another quirk which makes going out a less frequent occurrence than it might be is that going out becomes such a project; many couples tend to find it faintly ridiculous to go to all of the trouble to get a babysitter just to go down to the pub for a few beers. Well, it does seem vaguely silly to pay the babysitter more than the cost of the few beers! So often, going out becomes a blowing out, which it needn't be. It could just as well be a drive to a pub in another neighbourhood for an inexpensive meal out or a film . . . remember the cinema!

As I have suggested before, this is also a good time to make a resolution to join that evening class — no time like the present for starting or brushing up your French, for taking badminton lessons, or joining the local health or squash club.

If money is so tight — and there are no babysitting circles and no grannies nearby to babysit — that getting out in the evening means getting out separately, go out regardless. Don't forget, your job is twenty-four hours a day, seven days a week, with no holidays and no overtime. You do deserve *some* time off. So demand it!

PART III:
Year Two
and Beyond

16. Toddling

Toddling tots *are* beguiling. Their pudgy baby fat has dissolved into plump, dimpled limbs, their bright faces beam at the smallest delights, and they greet life with almost irrespressible joy. Small wonder that it is a rare toddler who is not genuinely beautiful and, therefore, appealing to all of those around him.

A toddler, at least in theory, is more willing to accept 'No', and to comply, than a younger baby. He may even be anxious to please, grabbing onto the handle of the vacuum cleaner or the mop to 'help' as you try to vacuum, bringing you tiny bits of fluff or paper from the carpet to put into the rubbish bin, shouting 'Mum! Mum! Mum!' at the fridge door whenever he wants a drink. In the second year of a baby's life there may be fewer milestones than during the first, such as eating solid food, sleeping through the night, weaning, sitting up, and crawling, but just as much dedicated devotion is required of a mother.

In fact, adorable as he may be, a toddler can be every bit as exhausting and tension-making as a crawling baby. Knowing what to expect should help to see you through.

Walking Toddlers

If a crawling baby is a potential catastrophe on all fours, a walking toddler is all that, but speeded up and with the added risk of his falling over, under, or off anything that he might climb onto. Multiply the problems of a crawler by an eighteen-inch reach and the ability to climb stairs, chairs, tables and also, I suspect, a fair knowledge of what he is not supposed to get into — if his quickness to enter forbidden territory the moment your back is turned is any indication.

This is the time to check your home again, mentally moving the height of your safety level up to whatever a toddler might reach by climbing onto a chair or a convenient table. Lock the medicine cabinet, keep washing-up liquid, dishwasher soap, and disinfectants very high indeed, preferably locked way (poisons should be locked in the garage or garden shed).

To give them their due, toddlers are a lot of fun and very companionable. Safely strapped into a harness, you can take them for *real* walks, but it is often necessary to trundle the pushchair along in case they get tired on the way home.

Trying to stroll through a supermarket or, heaven forbid, a toy shop, with a toddler restrained only by a harness, is simply asking for trouble. In shops, I have found the best plot is to keep the toddler in a pushchair or the childseat of the shopping trolley — carefully parking the trolley or pushchair in the middle of the aisle so that the shelves on either side are well out of his reach (you see, mothers aren't aisle-hogs!). Otherwise, just think of all the toys or the pretty juice bottles that he might pull off the shelves, not to mention sweets, if he has been allowed to discover their evil purpose! Even in the seat of the shopping trolley, you daren't turn your back or he might climb out. Harnesses don't seem to hold toddlers in that tightly.

Toddler at Large

At some point, usually sometime after it has been happening for a few weeks, a mother will suddenly realize that her toddler is more or less 'safe' in the house, that he has learned what he is to keep out of and off, and that she can actually turn her back for a moment to walk into another room, that she can go to the loo (if he will let her without standing at the door and banging or bellowing), and that she can answer the door without fearing for his life. Telephone calls still tend to be too long. You get to feel, instinctively, when a silence has become ominous, say, more than two minutes, and to go immediately to investigate how the toddler is occupying himself.

This is not to say that he still won't venture into forbidden realms. There are always tantalizing new frontiers to tempt him: make-up, toothpaste, crayons for wall murals, clothes to pull out of drawers. But the end of the worst — most demanding — period is approaching when you no longer have to be watchful every waking moment of the toddler's existence!

Adult Food

If a mother hasn't already mashed or liquidized adult foods for her child, so that he has become accustomed to the tastes, it is usually sometime between a child's first and second birthdays that a mother decides to convert the baby to 'real' food. This can be a traumatic time for all concerned, especially if the baby decides that he doesn't particularly want to move on from baby food.

Some children are easily converted; watching their parents eat toasted cheese, bread and paté, shepherd's pie, etc., induces them to have bites. Others — and one of mine was among the others — are lazy little so-and-so's who refuse to learn to chew, who insist upon swallowing any small lump of food whole, nearly choking themselves in the process, or washing every bite down liberally with milk.

When a child refuses outright even to try food which his mother has lovingly prepared for him, it is frustrating and maddening, and very difficult to obey the baby books which say, 'If a child won't eat, don't worry, just wait until the next meal.' I swear that my little girl lived on milk alone from the age of eighteen to twenty-four months. But eventually, even *she* got over the squirrel stage of storing food in her cheeks before swishing it all down with milk, so there is hope. And she kept growing all the time!

Feeding Themselves

There are several schools of thought about babies learning to feed themselves. One school says that almost as soon as the baby has accepted solid food, he ought to be allowed to try to help spoon it in, the baby holding one spoon and the mother another, which does the job. This hearty school of thought, which I have always privately termed 'the school of free expression', suggests putting down papers or a wipeable cloth under the highchair so that you don't have to mop the floor after every meal (not to mention launder your own clothes and shampoo the baby!) The proponents of this philosophy do not say what to do about the bowls that are flung across the room, plopped on top of the baby's head, or yours. . . .

When you decide to introduce the baby to his own spoon is up to you — and your nerves. Knowing that mine were already well frayed, by trying to entice the baby to eat *at all*, I decided on the restrictive practice of feeding her myself, bite by bite, never allowing her the opportunity to get a spoonful or handful of anything to throw unless I was reasonably certain that she was so keen to eat whatever was being offered that it would go where it was intended — try ice cream! But it doesn't seem to have harmed her. By two-and-a-half or three, she could manage anything bite-sized that would go into a spoon, and by four she had pretty well learned to manipulate a knife and fork with a little help in cutting.

Potty Training

Until fairly recently, the fashion in potty training was to get it over as early as possible, starting even before the baby had reached his first birthday! Now, the thinking is that trying too early is not so much training a baby (before his body is capable of control) as training the mother. The current trend is therefore to do it sometime between eighteen months and three, 'When the child is ready', as the books say.

Potty training is a delightful time when a mother becomes Mrs Mop, trailing around behind her toddler with a potty and a mop to clean up his puddles and worse. I know of only one mother who boasts that her child 'just decided to be dry'. Neither of mine did. More than a little auto-suggestion was necessary (understatement), and fairly persistent questioning: 'Would you like to sit on your potty now?' 'Come, sit on your potty now for a minute.' 'Do a nice wee-wee for Mummy.' Sometimes they hate sitting on the potty. I found that giving them a toy helped to keep them there, even if it was distracting.

With each of my children, we had several false starts. 'Potty train in the summer, if possible,' everyone says, so that they can run around without anything on and just wee in the grass. With each of mine I tried first at two years and three months, solidly for a fortnight, never scoring — not a single drop in the potty — before giving up. I tried a month later for another fortnight, and still no positive results. It helps to be able to stay at home all day when you are potty training, so that the child is not confused by what is expected if he is put into a nappy to go out.

With our first child, sweet success came — one wee in the potty — after staying at home for four days over a holiday weekend when she was two years and five months old. Our son was about the same age when he heard his mum's first squeals of delight: 'Good boy, what a good boy!' The secret, I am told, is to make *much* of the child's first success, and he or she will then try to please you again. The only difficulty, as you will have deduced, is reaching that first piddle. After that there is still a long way to go. I found that I had to keep asking the child about every fifteen minutes, putting each of them on the potty almost as frequently; still, there were countless accidents.

I know there is one school of thought that insists that if you really persist in doing *nothing else* but potty training, it can be accomplished in twenty-four to thirty-six hours. I've yet to meet anyone who has succeeded in that time. The whole procedure, from first introduction to the potty to the glorious day when you realize that you no longer have to carry the potty *everywhere* you go in order to produce it at an instant's notice, can take from two weeks to about six months. (I do know one mum who swears she accomplished it with her three-year-old son in two weeks! That's the quickest I know.) There is a lot of bending down and mopping up, so a wise woman doesn't plan it late in her next pregnancy!

Mobility

Toddlers love going places and seeing new things, but often tire rather quickly, so you still need to have the pushchair on hand for when a small voice announces, 'My little legs are tired.' Meal-times and nap times will still rule your planning, although a biscuit and a snorkel cup of milk in the car can often hold them for another half hour if the excursion takes longer than anticipated.

This is not the time to visit stately homes (other than their gardens), museums, galleries or exhibitions, unless fifteen minutes will do it. We have taken our toddlers through boat shows and motor shows; and as long as they were allowed, however briefly, to climb into one of the new cars or to clamber onto a real boat the day was a thrilling success. This is the time for zoos, safari parks, rides on miniature trains, and even a vintage car museum was a hit when it turned out to have a miniature racing car!

However it is not a particularly good time for lunching out until your toddler has responsibly mastered his spoon, or until throwing or dropping food overboard from the highchair is such a remote memory that you feel utterly secure in the faith that he won't do it. Otherwise, you are on tenterhooks, and not many restaurants have highchairs in this country anyway. The other *modus operandi* in a restaurant is to strap the toddler into his pushchair and to feed him, bite by bite, if he will suffer such indignity, or to stick to finger-food — tiny bite-sized sandwiches (cut up), buns, cakes, pasties, etc. Of course, pub gardens are much easier: there are no worries over crumbs, and no one cares if a toddler wanders around so long as he doesn't intrude on other people.

Throughout the toddler era, we have found that picnics — even picnics in the car in rainy weather — are great fun. If you have a soft upholstered backseat, it is a wise investment to protect it with a zip-on clear plastic cover from the time you install the carseat, and you are set for any mini-upsets or cake-crumbling.

From the moment a baby can walk, he will love to go for walks — in a safety harness if you are anywhere near traffic. Also, remember that he will still fall about a lot, so you have to think about what he will be falling onto or into when you decide to let him out of the safety harness. Let loose in a safe place, a park for instance, he will shoot off to investigate all of the brambles, puddles, dandelions and dog faeces within range. I will never forget the night at supper, after a lovely walk over moorland, when my husband asked our small daughter what she had seen on her walk — 'Poo!' she announced triumphantly.

With a bit of luck, your toddler may enjoy riding in the car, as long as there are stops about once an hour so that he can jump out and run around — longer if you judiciously plot your departure just in time for a nap.

Now that his focus is slightly higher off the ground, he will adore the beach. He will have stopped eating sand, except when sprinkled on his chocolate biscuit, and love shovelling it into his bucket and all over you and the blanket. He may be an investigator, wandering constantly so that you are forever retrieving him, or you may be lucky to have a toddler who sticks to you, digging his castles nearby. The chances are that he will be terrified of the coldness of the water when you first dangle his feet in, but once in, you will probably have to drag him out. I have spent whole afternoons trudging along the edges of the sea from one end of the beach to the other with a child who refused to leave the water, even for a bribe of ice cream! I've yet to meet a toddler who didn't adore the seaside. In fact, excursions to the beach, if there is one near enough to you, are fine for toddlers all year round. Just pull on wellies and off you go — one of your new liberties with toddlers, as opposed to crawlers who are too heavy to carry and whose pushchairs bog down in the sand.

17. Talking

It may be thrilling when your child's tiny voice first repeats 'Let's go', or first strings together the words, 'I wan' ice-cream'. A child's first attempts at communication can seem almost magical, so improbable it may seem that this small person can produce them. How often do you see a mother, father, or grandparent, coaxing a child to repeat a word — always a first child.

By the arrival of the second, parents have learned that the quickest route to hysteria, with milestones of absent-mindedness, frustration and screaming along the way, is teaching a toddler to talk — and responding to his endlessly repetitive, moronic questions. It is not an exaggeration to say that as a child learns to talk, the majority of a mother's consciousness during his waking day will become dominated by childish chatter.

Some children, like our first, develop their use of language very slowly, rather like the drip, drip of an irreparable tap. Our second, who waited to start to talk until we had nearly despaired of his being anything but backward, suddenly exploded into speech with whole phrases, complete with prepositions, if not articles — and after the mother-child relationship had become diluted by the respite of a nursery school, which makes the whole process a bit less intense. Whereas the first used to repeat the same infernal questions to infinity, the younger began to communicate from the first 'red car'. But the repetition is just as endless.

Unless you have ever experienced a chattering child, exploring language and exercising his awakening mind, you may find it impossible to imagine just how totally consuming, how utterly overwhelming it can be. As soon as a child can put two words together — 'Wha's 'at?' — vanished is your peace, not to mention your peace of mind and concentration, until nursery school or playgroup removes him from earshot for a few hours of the day.

This bombardment is mostly nonsensical, half-articulated, indistinct, and repetitive in the extreme; and it is always aimed at getting some kind of response from a mother, which is necessary if the child is going to learn to talk. But just fancy yourself trying to teach a foreign language without a break for at least twelve hours a day, every day, seven days a week. Then consider how much more demanding it is to teach not an adult, who approaches a language presumably, with some logic and motivation, but a monkey, which your child is not far off in ability, when you consider his undeveloped brain at this stage.

Although there must be a paragon of long-suffering patience somewhere, I have yet to meet a single full-time, stay-at-home mother, no matter how devoted, who during this period from roughly two or two-and-a-half, when her toddler starts asking questions, to about four when the questions finally begin to settle into some semblance of reason — (roll on the age of reason), who does not swear to having been slowly, mentally eroded into a twitching, screeching mass at one time or another! I personally can think of no worse mental torture than hour after hour of trying to converse, if that's the word, with a young child. Granted, I lack patience; you may have more. But even for the best of us, it is a trying time.

The first to hit you is the child's never-fail pat question: 'Why?' And it's no good just answering; the child will repeat the question, no matter how many times you satisfactorily reply.

The child is really getting to grips with his world when he branches out with questions like: 'Mummy, what's a hill?' 'What are clouds?' 'What's rain?' 'What's snow?' 'What are those white bits in the road?' The mind boggling repetition continues, even with more vocabulary at his disposal. A small child seems to be in love with the sound of his own voice, so incessantly does the chatter go on, and on, and on. Only in the blissful silence after a child finally sinks into his cot at night can a mother gather her shattered nerves and literally try to *collect her wits* — such clichés have taken on new meaning to me since mothering a talking toddler!

During this period of teaching a toddler to talk, making a super-human, self-denying effort, day after day to help the child along the way to rapid-fire speech, most mothers become terribly frustrated at not being left any time to themselves. A second cliché — *I don't even have time to think!* A mother can positively yearn for uninterrupted talk, and possibly intellectual stimulation from other consenting adults.

The disadvantage to mother-and-toddler groups during this period, or any other socializing that a mother might try with the toddler in tow, is that the child will act virtually as a buffer between his mother and any other adult. The child interrupts adult conversations so determinedly — long before he can be taught what an interruption is — that to carry on an adult conversation in his presence is well nigh impossible. This constant interruption leaves a mother unable to complete her thoughts, unable to have a reasonable conversation. Many mothers, stopped in mid-sentence by a child, are utterly unable to remember what they were even talking about. Most mothers of talking toddlers complain that they find it difficult to 'think straight', to follow any train of thought through to conclusion.

A mother may get home, say from a coffee morning, and realize that her frustration is not only that she has had to leap up and down to keep her toddler from damaging other people's belongings or babies — (any strange environment is a brand new world to be explored) — but because there has been so little chance to hold — and *hold* is the word — a conversation with anyone. Furthermore, the constancy of a toddler's chatter impedes most mothers from reading (naps are often by now a thing of the past), listening to the radio (except music), or watching anything but children's television programmes during the day while the child is awake. The child's incessant chatter cuts through all her thoughts, even if it is only making a grocery list.

This is often when a guilt trap springs on the unsuspecting mother. She wants to do the best for her child. She wants him to grow and develop, to help him to learn about his world, to speed him on his way, and how we try. Oh, how we try! We are all told how important talking and story-telling are later for pre-reading. So the devoted mother bends her efforts to encourage the toddler to chatter right up to her own breaking point — when she screams: 'For heavens sake, shut up!'

To say the least, a child finds this sudden shift of maternal attitude perplexing and hurtful. The only way to avoid reaching this crisis flash point is relief through escape.

Help!

Children's television programmes can help. If a child's attention is caught without the mother having to be present, she can escape to another room for the duration of a programme — at least fifteen minutes. I know that we are told that it is best for the child if we watch the programmes together, discussing them as they progress. Fine, for good days. For bad days, they offer a brief respite.

Daddy can also offer a bit of relief. If Daddy gets home early enough for him to catch a dose of childish chatter, just when he wants to tell you about his day, at least he'll understand your frustration, and the change from one adult to another will be good for the child, too — different ideas, new vocabulary, a fresh and interested audience. With a husband's support in taking on the chatterbox until the child's bedtime, the pressure is off just when a mother is apt to be at her lowest, and let's not forget, at her busiest, getting the evening meal on the table.

Another way to mitigate the chatter is to spread it amongst mothers with other chatterboxes. I know one woman who lives on an estate with communal gardens, and she and her neighbours take it in turns to watch the toddlers as they all play together, giving relief to the others on their off-days. Even if you do not have a communal garden, an informal rota system with three or four other mothers to have the children for a couple of mornings or afternoons a week helps a great deal. And the socializing is good for the children.

To say that this is a time when your adult social life is crucial is an understatement. Getting out and away from the toddler, preferably with your husband, is equally crucial — to your marriage — not to mention your mental health! Why else do you think that so many mothers of young children are on tranquillizers? It isn't that they are faint-hearted or lacking in moral fibre. It's just that certain periods during a young child's development are excruciatingly harrowing for the person looking after him, if it's on a one-to-one basis. Obviously tranquillizers are not the answer. They only mask the symptoms. A better approach is to try to control the causes of the anguish — too much constant toddler talk!

Apart from his chattering, a mother is at the child's constant command. Compare child rearing to looking after a nearly helpless invalid. No one would expect anyone to be at the invalid's beck and call all day, every day, without any breaks, not even going into the next room! But the invalid, though possibly cantankerous and tetchy, is at least a more or less reasonable, rational adult. Not so a toddler! He's unreasonable and irrational in the extreme.

You have doubtless heard that old adage: all work and no play makes Jack a dull boy. Well, I think it holds for mums too: all childish chatter makes mum a 'chatter-brain'. I could name at least a dozen chatter-brained mums, tense and depressed from not having sufficient escape hatches, and I suspect that the phenomena is widespread during the pre-school years.

In an opinion poll published by *The Sunday Times* (2 May 1982), which asked for reactions to the statement: 'Women with young children should not go out to work but should stay at home to look after them,' there was the following result:

> A 61 percent majority of all respondents agreed more or less strongly (with women alone registering a somewhat weaker vote). But interestingly enough, in the detailed breakdown by age, it was the 25 to 35-year-olds — the parents who preponderantly have the young children to look after — who registered the strongest disagreement. In fact, in that particular group, the answers came out almost level pegging — 42 per cent in favour of undiluted motherly care, and *39 per cent for getting some sort of change from dependence and nursery conversation.*

Escaping back into the adult world, even for short forays, is terribly important for any sense of balance and well-being. As I have suggested before, evening courses are a good, cheap way of committing yourself to a regular hour of concentrating on something other than the children. The National Housewives' Register, or the National Childbirth Trust both provide free nights out with other like-minded women.

It's also a good idea to plot little projects for yourself now and again to keep your self-esteem afloat: trying a new recipe after the children are in bed, making a dress or knitting a pullover for yourself or your child, drawing or painting, or writing — even if it's only letters. Or do you like reading (magazines or a good novel) or working in the garden? Tired as you may be after tucking a child in, it's nice to feel that you can 'do your own thing' sometimes, instead of just sagging on the settee in front of the box.

But do give yourself some time off! I know when I walk out of the house and close the door behind me, it's like not banging my head against the wall anymore. The silence is that sublime. The pressure is off, and I can be *me* and not *Mummy* for a while.

Retaining Your Self-esteem

Unless you guard against it, the constant intellectual knock-down, delivered over a period of two or three years with each child, can accumulate and translate itself, almost inevitably, into lowered self-esteem. It works in the following way:

A full-time mother, under the constant barrage of trivial talk from her offspring, until she can hardly keep her mind on whatever she is meant to be doing, in fact, does not — cannot — perform as well as she once did, before having a child or children. It is only with determination, given the constant assault of thought-interrupting chatter, that she can concentrate on housework, cooking, or skimming a newspaper. Most women complain that they find it terribly difficult to keep abreast of what's going on. You're lucky to get any sense out of the television news with a shrieking toddler at your elbow.

It is equally difficult for a woman to keep up with new developments in her previous professional field. Even if she has no plans whatsoever to return to her job, she may feel herself slipping out of touch professionally. Where formerly she may have been well-organized and orderly, or perhaps disorganized but creative, her entire self-image will have to be altered. She is no longer mistress of her life. She is unable now to undertake many of the tasks or projects she once would have accomplished easily. Add to that the fact that she is having to work more slowly (children never hurry), at lowered efficiency (because of interruptions), day in and day out, and naturally, quite correctly, she feels that she is not doing anything quite as well as she once did.

Leaving any intellectual outlet aside, look at the domestic front for a moment. A mother is usually the person who looks after the household administration: planning the meals, shopping for food and clothing, cooking, taking anything to be repaired and clothes to be dry cleaned, doing washing and ironing, the cleaning, sometimes gardening, and often paying the household bills. If it's done well, it is certainly a full-time job, at least it is to the standard to which I aspire — on a guilt-ridden day.

Mothering is also a full time job: if it is for a nanny, it is for a child's natural mother. Add the two together — taking into consideration that looking after a child, toddling off into danger, or constantly chattering to her as she sits down to write cheques — and the end product is that she is unable to fulfil either role very satisfactorily. It is an ideal recipe for dissatisfaction, guilt, and lowered self-esteem; hence the need for other outlets that provide some sense of accomplishment. If a woman is not really able to point to anything that she feels that she is doing very well, it is no wonder she feels a loss of self-respect, not to mention the status she has lost by becoming 'a housewife and mother'.

It doesn't matter much that any of her household tasks, taken alone, is quite easy. In fact, knowing that makes it rather worse, that she is not even able to be a good cook or housekeeper, for instance. It is trying to do everything at once, with the constant interruptions of a child that can get to her in the end. It is very tempting to sink into a masochistic mire of depression, to feel that you are unable to accomplish anything that you would like to and, worst of all, that no one appreciates anything that you do try to do.

Not a child in the world has ever thanked his mother for putting his clothes on in the morning or for taking him to the swings — the child only yells when he is taken away. Husbands don't thank their wives for vacuuming, or for looking after the baby! Perhaps we should thank *them* for going to work every day, at least once in a while. A little mutual appreciation goes a long way . . . .

But I digress. To be sure, the job a mother held down before having children may not have provided much appreciation of her efforts, but it might at least have given her a feeling of having *completed* something now and then. Motherhood and housewifery go on and on, and don't give you many such feelings of accomplishment, unless you get a real kick out of a clean house. Even that is denied to most mothers, because it is simply not safe to lock the (screaming) child in one room while they finish the rest of the house. It never stays tidy in one area long enough for a woman to stand back and admire her work.

So plot your own salvation, be it an escape to a course in wholefood cookery, an evening of squash with your husband, or a craft project at home — anything to give *you* a change, some time off from child-nurturing and, as a bonus, perhaps a feeling of having accomplished something.

And remember, there is life after children . . . .

18. The Second Child

We thought for a long time before deciding to have a second child. At forty-one, I felt rather old to have a baby: the risks were greater, and with our first child just coming up to two, we knew that we were over the worst of the nappies, bottles, baby food, prams and pushchairs. Knowing what to expect the second time, it took more than a deep breath to contemplate starting all over again. More importantly, I felt a lurking fear that, so besotted had I been with our first child, I could never love another baby quite as much.

For several months we pondered. At last we decided to try, mainly on the grounds that it was unfair to leave our firstborn alone in the world. Both my husband and I, as only children, remembered the loneliness of growing up alone. And our little daughter, once her grandparents and parents were gone, would have no aunts or uncles, no cousins to turn to — no family left at all.

A few months later, when the chemist's pregnancy test showed positive, we were elated. It hadn't been too late. Yet at the same time, I felt a noose of commitment tighten around my throat. Here we go again, I thought, tied to a tight regime of baby-care for another three years.

As with my first pregnancy, when the time came, I had the tests for spina bifida and mongolism. The results, agonizingly held up by the Christmas holidays, finally came through clear, 'and the sex of your baby is male'. I had to read the letter again, I was so taken aback. Somehow, emotionally, I had been all set for another little girl. I knew about little girls, I liked little girls. Now, all those pretty, frilly dresses that I had been so carefully putting aside as our firstborn grew out of them could not be used; well, I would have to find a friend with a little girl. My husband, of course, was pleased. A boy to garden with, to go fishing with, to play football with; although I kept reminding him that girls like doing all of those things, too!

The first four months of the pregnancy went so smoothly and quickly that for most of it I had a secret dread that I wasn't really pregnant. The last few months dragged, none longer than the last few weeks as I kept getting sharp pains and thinking that any day, any hour, labour would begin, and then whoopee, it would be over.

As each day overdue dragged on, and each night passed uneventfully, I began to worry. When a week had passed, the doctor agreed that perhaps I should come into hospital. I put it off for another two days. Then, under threat of induction, ten days later, the lump finally began to move!

The Second New Arrival

Mothers always tell you how much more relaxed they were with the second than with the first. What they don't tell you is how much more fraught it is looking after two, (or three, or four) young children, than just one. No matter how much gentle preparation you make, explaining to the first child that a baby is on the way, and no matter how delighted he may seem at the whole idea, the actual appearance of the new baby may still come as a shock to his world.

When Granny brought our little daughter to visit that first afternoon at the maternity home, she hung back, holding onto Granny's hand and refused to come to me. That hurt terribly. When at last she was lifted onto the bed for a cuddle, she remained terribly quiet, as though she knew that nothing would ever be quite the same.

As the days passed, her visits became an emotional trial. I felt dreadfully tired and weak, and the stitches were so painful that I dared not lift her. Keeping her occupied for the duration of the visiting period, no matter what toys were brought in, seemed beyond my physical capacity.

Eventually, though it tore my heart to do it, I had to suggest to Granny that she bring her in for only twenty minutes at a time, and that worked better. But it didn't help that she never minded leaving me with Granny every day. Instead of *her* feeling rejected, it was *me* who was feeling rejected by my dear, beloved child.

The evening the baby and I came home from the maternity home, a day I had been eagerly awaiting, was heart-breaking. When Granny brought our daughter home, she cried and cried, not wanting Granny to leave. She pushed me away, crying for Granny. After all, *I* had abandoned her! I wept myself to sleep that night. I understood her anger, her rejection, but I felt that I had irretrievably lost something very precious — the love and trust of our first child.

During those first few weeks at home, I seemed to do nothing but feed the baby all day — five hours of suckling, winding and changing — which caused conflict with our daughter. I was always feeding him whenever her shoes came magically unbuckled, orange juice or a biscuit were required, or dolly's dress needed its bow tied. I found myself getting very cross with her. I was still terribly tired, and to get up out of the chair and put the baby down, heavy lump that he was, and to attend to whatever request she might have in the middle of a feed, seemed too much to ask.

I understood *why* it was happening. In her way, she was seeking the reassurance of mummy's love through attention; but being human, I resented her not trying to be her usual, imaginatively helpful self just when I needed her help most. And then, there was this plump lump towards whom I didn't feel very much, who was causing all the angst!

Regression

Regression usually comes immediately. Once a new baby is home and starts to monopolize his mother's time, which previously was devoted entirely to the older child, he naturally feels the loss of his mother's attention. He usually reacts accordingly, making almost impossible demands upon his mother to prove her undying affection — just when she is at her lowest, weary from the night feeds and still recovering from the delivery.

The toddler cries at invented tumbles; he may revert to making baby gurgling noises; and if all else fails, he may resort to thumping the new baby, or kicking and screaming tantrums. One toddler I know, poor child, confidentially told her father that she'd be much happier 'when the baby goes back'.

If the toddler has come through potty training, he is liable to start having accidents again, just when his poor mother least feels able to mop up puddles, and worse — if he finds that puddles don't merit sufficient response.

What a toddler needs, we are told, is lots of extra cuddling and reassurance that his mother still loves him, no matter how naughty he might be. But goodness, it *is* asking sainthood of a woman, who is dead tired, to contain her temper and stretch her patience, and to speak to the recalcitrant toddler in dulcet, soothing tones, telling him what a sweet child he is and how he is mummy's little darling when he has deliberately distributed a bowel movement from the sitting room to the kitchen!

Coping with Two

This period from a new baby's homecoming until he starts to sleep through the night, when the mother can regain some of her strength and equanimity, and the number of the baby's feeds are reduced (so that the toddler no longer feels that mummy is totally monopolized by this newcomer) is not just a time for rejoicing! More than ever, a woman needs the help of her husband to take the children off her hands so that she can rest.

Having an older child around, who may be past nap-taking by the time the second arrives (as I have discussed before), means that a mother has little chance during the day to drop into bed to catch up on sleep. The predictable result is that it takes her longer to recoup after the birth of a second child than the first. By evening, she is so tired that she drops into bed immediately after supper, so that she sees little of her husband. During the weekends, when he is at home, she literally falls into bed to try to recoup some of the sleep that she has been losing throughout the week.

Getting Help

But there are ways of alleviating the strain of coping during these first few weeks at home with a new baby and a toddler.

If you can possibly afford to, hire someone to do the cleaning, laundry and ironing. Help is even more necessary after the birth of a second baby than the first — at least for a few weeks or months until the end of the night feeds. If you can't afford help, trim the domestic chores to an absolute minimum, and hopefully, your husband will help.

It certainly helps if a mother, before the new baby's arrival, can manage to dilute her attention to the firstborn by widening his environment and the people of importance in it, so that the appearance of the newborn will not leave him feeling that his one-to-one world with mummy has shattered.

Grandparents can help by asking him to spend a day with them, or even a few hours, on a regular basis, starting well before the arrival of the new baby so that he doesn't feel that he is being pushed out of the nest.

This is also a good time for the toddler to set off with Daddy to work in the garden, or to do whatever Daddy likes doing. It can be a rewarding time for Daddy to discover the fun of a one-to-one relationship with his older child.

A mother might exchange babysitting with a friend, one morning or afternoon a week, or even a whole day, so that when the new baby comes, the older child has another world to go to that he already knows and enjoys.

The same theory holds for settling a toddler, if possible, into a nursery school or playgroup well before the appearance of the new baby: this avoids making him feel that he is being pushed out, just when the newcomer arrives, if he is old enough to be accepted at the playgroup.

Likewise, if the older child has become well acquainted with a babysitter before the arrival of a new baby, hiring the babysitter for perhaps one afternoon during the week can give the mother a chance for some much needed rest, and a quicker period of recuperation.

Involving the Older Child

It helps if you can involve the older child in looking after his new brother or sister by asking him to fetch the baby powder or a clean nappy, to pick up a dropped bootee, and by letting him touch, cuddle and even hold the baby (with help) on his lap. You can also try sitting the toddler beside you with a book to read to him while the baby feeds (quite a juggling act, but not impossible).

A mother may try very hard, but regression can still be a recipe for mutual misery as she attempts to satisfy the needs of both children simultaneously. Against this background of a mother's exhaustion, add the toddler's mindless chatter, along with the baby's occasional insistent, inexplicable crying, and it is easy to see why mothers of new babies and toddlers feel harrassed.

Guilt

Apart from the problems of tiredness and regression, this can be a guilt-ridden time. First, a mother may feel guilty and torn between the needs of her two children. I have often heard mothers discussing this inner conflict with questions like: 'If they both cry at once, which one do you go to?' One mother answered: 'To the older child because he will realize that you are making a choice, whereas the younger won't.' Another said, 'To the youngest because he might suffocate if he cries so hard that he vomits and chokes', but she rapidly followed this by explaining how she would pick up the baby and go immediately to the toddler to comfort him.

A good many mothers feel that they are somehow betraying their love for their firstborn just by having a second child — almost like taking another lover, the guilt is that intense. Furthermore, they feel equally guilty towards the second child because they fear that they may never be able to love him quite as much as the first.

Looking back on the arrival of our own second child, as ridiculous as it may seem, I came to enjoy the night feeds. Alone with the baby, I could give him my unguarded affection, cooing and cuddling him, singing, and making clicking noises, which he enjoyed. He was a very warm, round little lapful and, at last, he learned to grasp one of my fingers in his plump, dimpled hand.

As he began to respond, slowly, so did I.

During the day, the heart-wrenching conflict with my daughter went on, as I recall, nearly until our baby elephant started to eat solid food at four months old, simultaneously cutting down the number of his feeds to three a day and one at night. This enabled me to eliminate virtually all but one feed from our daughter's existence.

She was asleep during his night and breakfast feeds, at nursery school during his lunch, and only present for his evening feed. I began to relax more and to enjoy him during those separate feeds. It also helped that he went to bed at night an hour or so before she did, so that she had Mummy to herself for a time.

Meanwhile, our little girl developed into quite the little mother with her dolly: up came her dress to breast-feed and the dolly had to have nappies and a cardigan to keep her warm, just like baby brother. She even began to be endearingly helpful with the baby — fetching nappies, bringing clean shirts and terrycloth suits at bath time. She loved to stretch up, standing on tiptoe to plant a goodnight kiss on his cheek.

It was just when I thought she was settling down to having the baby around that she came up one day when I was feeding him, pointed to the other breast and said, 'Ashley's, Ashley wants some, too.'

My heart sank. I'd heard of regression, but for a nearly three-year-old to sink back to suckling babyhood! 'Did you let her?' a friend asked later. 'That would have cured it.' But at the time, I had been so shaken that it had never occurred to me to let her. Afterwards, the moment had passed. She contented herself with feeding dolly.

Mothers may also feel guilty that with the arrival of a new baby, they have less time to play with, to chat to, to read stories to, and to encourage their older children in their development. It is inevitable. There is only so much time left over after the feeding, changing and bathing of the baby, after the laundry, preparing the meals for herself, her husband, and the toddler. A mother can only try to make sure that her firstborn enjoys her company for at least one or two short periods while the baby is asleep, every day.

Aggression

If regression does not appear immediately — not until the new baby starts to sit up and reach for the older child's toys, or perhaps not even until the new baby starts to crawl after toys — count yourself lucky. At least you will have more strength to cope with the traumas than if you were recovering from the delivery and the night feeds.

Aggresssion can strike anytime, either the older child punching or scratching the baby, or the younger one at the older — believe me, as soon as a baby can sit up, he can hit and viciously pull hair! I'm still waiting for the aggression to subside, and mine are two and four.

How you handle it depends on what you and your husband have mutually decided. Do you leave them to it and let them sort it out? It seems hardly fair given the difference in physical strength and mobility. Do you pull them apart and make the (older) offender apologize — if he's capable — explaining that he can have a turn with the toy later?

If it is the younger who is the offender, you haven't a chance in heaven of making a sitting baby understand what 'your turn later' means, or even probably, that he is being naughty. He's not; he's just acting naturally to try to get what he wants in a fairly clever way of getting it! So, do you smack the young offender's hand, explaining that it is wrong to pull his sister's hair, hoping that he will eventually understand?

As soon as a baby can sit up and reach, you will have to limit some toys — dangerous ones for the little one to swallow — to one child; but explaining the rights of possession, I warn you, is totally lost on sitting (and most crawling) babies.

Certainly, an area where the older child righteously can feel aggrieved is when a good many of his toys have to be put out of reach of the baby because tiny parts might go into the baby's mouth and be swallowed. It takes a lot of picking up, sorting out, and putting away in the course of a day to make sure that no tiny eatable objects are left where the baby can get hold of them. But at least, this comes after a mother has recovered from the loss of sleep and the delivery, when the new baby has established his position in the family.

I tried keeping the more dangerous toys in the older child's room 'to play with while the baby is asleep', but it seemed hard to forbid her from playing with many of her own toys whenever the baby was around, which doubtless added fuel to the older child's resentment of the baby. A mother can feel that segregating the toys is arresting the older child's development, but it *is* the only really safe solution.

Mobility

Now that baby makes four, outings with two young children have to be arranged to fit around both children's needs for feeding and naps, which is not as easy as fitting around the needs of one. Shopping trips for food or clothes, for you or for the children, can take on the tactical plottings of an expedition, and exquisite timing to avoid the alarm bell — the baby's crying — going off in the middle of a busy shop.

If you have the pram fitted with one of those little seats for the toddler on top (as long as the toddler isn't too heavy), you daren't leave the pram unobserved for a moment, either in a supermarket or a boutique, for fear that the toddler might unbalance the pram by leaning over to reach for something.

With a pushchair and the toddler on reins, the occupant of the pushchair is likely to revolt vocally if his older brother or sister is shown favouritism by being allowed into the changing cubicle with Mummy while he is left outside, rejected! But you can't rely on the older child to stay by the pushchair while you pop in to try on that new bikini! He might wander off anywhere, and the public don't think much of mothers who tie their children to pushchairs with reins, even if it is for their own safety. Really it is best to do shopping for clothes for yourself with Dad or a friend along to keep the children busy, while you disappear into the fitting rooms.

Of course, if your babies are sufficiently close together, you can use a double pushchair, but work out how long the older child will actually use it (normally until a bit over three years), before deciding to buy this rather expensive piece of equipment. The advantage of a double pushchair is that you can lower the back and the youngest can sleep as you go along. The disadvantages are that they are heavy to push, especially uphill, and an unnecessary encumbrance once you are using it for only one child after the toddler has started nursery school or playgroup, unless you still have a leftover single pushchair.

Going to the beach on your own, with a baby and a toddler, is for the intrepid; but as long as the baby is sitting and not yet crawling, it is not an impossible feat. There *is* a lot of clobber for one person to carry, plus also having to hang onto two youngsters: nappy bag, bottles and cups and thermoses of drinks, a snack for you and them, toys, the beach blanket and, if you are wise, in England a wind-break. If you have the sort of pushchair that folds back so that the baby can sleep, you can dangle some of these bags from the handles, but careful, once you hit the soft sand, pushchairs tend to bog down and easily tip over.

Once your youngest is crawling, I have to remind you that crawling babies love nothing better than eating sand, seaweed, shells and pebbles. Chasing a toddler and a crawler in opposite directions is no way to get a sun tan! I have found that you need at least one adult for each child, and an extra adult or two is not unwelcome if you hope to build a sand castle! More than one adult is more fun for the toddler, as well. When one adult wearies of tossing the ball, he can move on to the next.

19. Travelling with Children

Young Babies

Fortunately, you can take a small baby almost anywhere. Like a turtle, he takes his familiar environment — his carrycot — with him, and as long as you are nearby to feed, change and cuddle him, his world is complete, no matter where you choose to move it. He will usually settle in a strange place, providing he is put down according to the same pattern as at home.

As a rule of thumb, the younger the baby, the easier he is to pack up and take for a jaunt. Looking back on your unencumbered past, this may not be immediately obvious. There may seem to be lot of clobber to pack; but there is much less while a baby is on breast milk or a formula than later when he starts eating solid food. Up to the age of about four months old, when most babies begin to eat solids, all you need are a plentiful supply of disposable nappies (from home or bought at your destination), the baby's clothes and bedding, his carrycot and wheels.

The only trouble is that often a mother doesn't really feel up to organizing even this small amount until the baby starts to leave off the night feeds. Unfortunately, that usually coincides with when he starts solid food, which means carting the food along, too.

In theory, anytime up to, and also during that period between solid food (four months) and weaning (six months), are ideal times for a holiday. Between four and six months old, the baby usually has begun to settle into a pattern of only three or four feeds a day, you have more time between his more predictable feeds for sightseeing or touring, and as long as you reach your destination in time for his early evening feed and put him down at the same time as at home, he's happy.

While I was expecting our first baby, my husband and I went on what we considered to be our last carefree holiday before the children (and how right we were!). At our hotel was a couple with their baby of only a few weeks old, and I remember thinking how clever the mother had been to have planned it so that the holiday would fall well after the baby was born, even if it had arrived late, but soon enough after the birth to give her some relief from the housekeeping. Furthermore, she had the additional bonus of having daddy there to take the baby for walks every day so that she could catch a nap now and again . . . beside the pool! My hat went off to this woman as she donned a loose maternity bathing suit to do her post-natal exercises lying on a deckchair! Disposable nappies solved most of her laundry problems, and the baby was breast-feeding; so all she needed were the baby's clothes, bedding, carrycot and wheels.

With hindsight, now that my youngest has reached toddlerhood, I realize how much easier it is to fly with a baby still in a carrycot — preferably before he starts solid foods — rather than a few months later when he has grown out of the carrycot, sits on your lap and wriggles, gets tired and fretful, and there is no place for him to lie down to sleep. But maybe your baby happily sleeps on your lap?

After a baby has started solid food, it is wise to take along the food to which he is accustomed. Unless he is an unusually hungry baby and eats anything put before him, why risk his rejecting new foods. Give yourself a rest.

On planes, the stewardess will provide baby food, if warned in advance, and keep your formula bottles cold; but if you bring your own dehydrated food, you will also need to bring a thermos of hot boiled water as there is no drinking water available on planes. In any case, if you take dehydrated foods you will need a small thermos so that you can ask for hot, boiled water to mix it with at your destination (it cools in a minute or two), and to save trouble, I always took the baby's own plastic bowl and spoon.

In hotels, we found it a good plot to feed the baby upstairs in our room before our own mealtime, and then to wheel the pram into the hotel dining room with a sated, sleepy baby (if there was no baby-listening service) for an uninterrupted leisurely meal.

Once a baby is weaned, you will need about a pint of cow's milk every day (and the bottles, nipples, sterilizing tablets and container). In Britain, getting his usual milk is easy. But find out if a cruise ship, for instance, uses powdered milk when you book. Babies don't like change, especially in anything as basic as their milk, and tend to react accordingly. Abroad, the milk often tastes a bit odd, due to different processing. We once found that our daughter simply wouldn't drink the milk (in Tenerife). We had to give her diluted fresh orange juice, and make sure that she had plenty of ice cream . . . she didn't seem to mind. It is important, especially in hot climates, to ensure that a baby or young child takes in sufficient liquid to avoid becoming dehydrated.

Crawlers

Once a baby is crawling, travelling becomes one degree more difficult. A crawler will simply not like being confined to a carseat, or having to sit on your lap (in a plane, for example), for very long before he wants to get down and crawl about. Also, having reached what I call the age of discrimination, at about eight months old, he will take notice of and object, usually, to being put down if mummy tries to leave him alone in a strange room.

By the time a baby is crawling, he has also developed a taste for a variety of foods, which means, quite a bundle of boxes or tins to take along if you are going abroad and are unsure of their availability.

Perhaps you are braver — or more determined — than I am but looking back I think it was wise not to have tried any too adventurous, long trips while the baby was at the crawling, and still very unreasonable, stage. With a toddler, you have a fighting chance of explaining that the plane will land soon, or that the bus will arrive at your hotel in only fifteen minutes — not that a toddler has any concept of time whatsoever, but a mother's reassurance might be accepted — while a crawling baby will simply shriek the house down when he gets over-tired.

We have found that it does help to set out, if it is a long car journey, long enough after the baby's feed for the food to have settled, but preferably, just when he would normally be due for a nap. If you buy a 'winged' childseat, they are quite comfortable and will support a sleepy little head as it lolls to one side. In fact, often the hum of an engine will send a crying baby off to sleep when nothing else will!

Usually it is sometime before a baby starts to crawl that he outgrows his carrycot. At home, he will graduate to a cot. For travelling, if you do it frequently and to destinations where you cannot be sure of finding a cot, a fold-up travel cot is the answer. But like anything new, it is wise to get the baby used to it at home before dropping him into it as a big surprise on the first night of your travels, at the end of a long tiring day, when you and your husband will not want to spend the evening with a baby who cries every time you try to leave the room.

If an ordinary cot is available at your destination, most mothers I know still bring along the baby's own bedding and a cuddly toy to give him a comfortable feeling of familiarity. Any bribery to keep him quiet and let you have some well earned peace!

Standing Babies and Toddlers

Climbing out of a travel cot is a cinch; this is not to say that you shouldn't use one, but you will need to play it by ear with your own child. If he has been accustomed to sleeping in one occasionally, he may be willing to continue sleeping in it, even knowing that he is able to get out. If he insistently climbs out every time you put him into it (sigh), you have the option of lying down with him to get him off to sleep, going only where there is a proper cot (provided he doesn't climb out of that), or settling him into an adult bed — after which he can always climb out. As you will appreciate, this doesn't leave you much peace of mind unless you stay within hearing.

Apart from the logistics, a toddler severely limits the activities of his parents on holiday. Gone are the touring holidays (with a carrycot baby) when adults could take pot luck in finding hotel accommodation. The toddler will not tolerate long periods in the car, and not all hotels cater — or even allow — young children to stay. Also, when you are travelling with a toddler, there is so much to pack that it is better to stay at least a week in each place.

A short list of the clobber that you will need must include: nappies (disposable if they are unavailable at your destination), even if he has graduated to potty training, at least for the nights; baby food (dry is lightest and takes least space) unless he has moved on to adult food — and he may reject strange, foreign food; a thermos for hot water if you use dried foods; a juice squeezer if your child prefers fresh juice and you are uncertain if it is available where you are going; possibly a stairguard; a pushchair; clothes for all eventualities — and toys. To limit the number of toys to too few is merely asking for trouble: you end up going out to buy more.

Having said all that, if you are well-armed with a variety of inexpensive new toys for a longish journey by car, bus, train, or plane, usually a toddler will be happy and charm all the granny-aged passengers in sight.

Perhaps I should mention here that touring bus holidays are out. Completely out: Even the tour operators have recognized that young children are not happy to sit immobile for long hours, possibly for several days. As a result, most tour companies prohibit children on bus tours until they are at least twelve.

Visiting Friends and Relatives

As suggested earlier, while a baby is very young it is a good time to visit friends and relatives, who are eager to see the new baby. It is less of an effort for you to be a guest in their homes than it is for you and your husband to have to entertain them in yours, just when you are juggling a lot of new tasks under a load of fatigue.

If the budget won't stretch to a holiday, even a weekend away can give you a psychological boost, just when your spirits might be apt to plummet at the end of those first two or three weeks at home — after your husband or helper goes back to work or home, and you are suddenly left to cope on your own with the new baby.

Once the baby is crawling, either you will have to make sure that there is a cot for the baby to sleep in, or take a portable cot with you. Obviously, you will need to make a rapid reconnaissance of the house on arrival, to remove all low, breakable objects. It is wise to bring your own stairguard if the household is childless. And is there an open fire? Unfortunately, babies never seem to take holidays from their desperate research into the new unknown, so taking a crawling baby with you is not very relaxing.

Once a toddler has left his cot, an extra bed is necessary at your destination, or a mattress on the floor, or a campbed. Plus lots of fascinating toys!

Farmhouses

While our first child was still in a carrycot, we had a very pleasant holiday early one September, staying in farmhouses which offered bed and breakfast and evening meals. The evening meal is important, because taking a sleeping infant in a pram into restaurants in this country requires steel nerves: they are simply not geared to children. It's much less hassle to park the carrycot upstairs in the farmhouse while you have your meal downstairs with an ear cocked to hear if the baby wakes up. And if the farmer's wife realizes that your baby goes off to sleep easily, she may volunteer to babysit one evening so that you can have a meal out.

Our original plan was to move from farmhouse to farmhouse each night, visiting stately homes up and down the length of the country, but even with guidebooks telling us where suitable farmhouses were located, there were several blank areas geographically, and despite what we thought was good forward planning, once or twice we found ourselves still searching for a farmhouse when the baby's feed time was due. There is nothing like an insistent wail from the back seat to upset the best laid plans: stop, give the baby a feed, a change, settle him back into the carrycot, and by then you may be cutting it very close to reach the farmer's wife in time for her to prepare your own supper. It only took once for us to start to book the farmhouses ahead, sight unseen, and to remain at each a minimum of a couple of nights just to avoid the daily trauma of resettling. Even better, probably, is a week in each (and there are often cheaper weekly rates).

Once your baby is crawling or walking, the same holds true for breakable objects, stairguards, sometimes fireguards, and constant vigilance in farmhouses, as for visiting friends and relatives.

One tip however: when booking a farmhouse do make sure, if your baby still needs an afternoon nap, that the farmer's wife doesn't mind your coming back after lunch. Some farmhouses expect you to be out from breakfast to tea time, which can be hard on a child who has outgrown a carrycot and finds it difficult to sleep in a pushchair or carseat.

Self-catering

Another cheap solution is to self-cater, be it in a cottage, a flat, or a caravan. It is no relief from the cooking, but a change, anyway. With a very young baby (who is not yet addicted to the beach), it doesn't much matter whether you go in the high season or just a bit before or after, so this is the time to take economic advantage of your situation. May and June can be just as hot and sunny (or rainy!) at the seaside in this country as July and August, so you may as well take a chance (as you will anytime) and pay less.

If you enquire when booking the cottage or flat, there may even be a babysitter available. Otherwise, if you have friends who also have a baby of about the same age, it can be fun to team up and go together, to share a larger cottage or flat, or to take caravans side by side. This provides adult company in the evenings, and you might trade off babysitting so that each couple can go out in turns. Though two families sharing the same accommodation doubtless adds to the domestic confusion, by sharing the cooking and washing up, the load can seem lighter — and a laugh.

With crawlers and toddlers, self-catering can be rather fraught. Although there may be several adults around to share the child-minding, somebody must be on *constant watch*. Leave the door ajar and in a twinkling the baby can slip outside into a fenced garden, or one that is unfenced with a steep-banked stream at the bottom. Flats are almost always coincidental with stairs (you need the stairguard), and caravan parks . . . I leave you to your own imagination.

Camping

A camping or caravan holiday is popular with many families, with no precious surroundings to destroy, no noise limitations, the feeding of children when they are hungry rather than when a hotel schedules children's tea and plenty of wide open space to romp in. But with a crawler or a toddler, one adult (preferably in turns) has to keep watch to make sure that the child doesn't wander off, make a nuisance of himself in somebody else's tent or caravan, or get into any possibly harmful mischief.

As I suggested before, a good solution is to join forces with another couple or two.

I must admit that camping, to my mind, is for the hearties who are already experienced — in this country. Remember that bad weather can make what should have been an idyllic retreat into the countryside, a cold, miserable and muddy nightmare. Add a crying baby, and most of us would load up and go home. But don't let me put you off altogether. If you are an ardent camper and have like-minded friends, who also have a carrycot-aged baby, join forces and carry on. If you are on your own the chances of finding a babysitter on a campsite are next to nil, and you will be stuck listening to a portable radio, watching a battery-operated television, reading or playing Monopoly by lamplight, or even *talking* to your spouse every evening while the other campers rush off to restaurants and pubs. It can make you feel rather left out.

Camping abroad, theoretically, should be slightly better in that you don't have to buy all of the camping equipment and then find that you hate it. Nor do you have to put it up yourself, or pack and hump it along with you to the campsite. Many camp sites abroad have three-bedroomed tents, fully equipped with everything but bedding and, if you go in high season, provide very appetizing carry-out meals in the evening (in France), I am told. Also, there is a better chance, further south, that the weather will be warm.

Hotels

Here or abroad, hotels are a relaxing solution — a break from the cooking — and as long as there is a lift, relatively easy with a young baby still in a carrycot. You can wheel the baby into the lift and go up without waking him. Provided there is a baby-listening service to let you off the twenty or thirty-minute check to make sure that he is asleep and all right, you can have a fairly easy mind about propping up the hotel bar and enjoying the floor show while the baby snoozes upstairs. Some hotels abroad even provide baby-patrols — someone to poke a head in and make sure that the baby is asleep and breathing. But it can be a problem to get the baby off to sleep, waiting in the darkened room until he (or you) falls asleep, before tiptoeing out for a fashionably late dinner.

Even *with* a baby-listening service, of course, you will have to hire a babysitter (if there is one available) to sit with the baby in your room should you want to leave the hotel for the evening.

Once a baby can stand up, holding onto something for support, he may try to climb out of whatever cot you put him into, his own, a travel cot, or someone else's. So it becomes one degree riskier to travel with a child once he can stand up. I would go so far as to say that once he can stand up in his cot, you must either have a baby-listening service in the room, stay within hearing in case he tries to climb out — or hire a babysitter to stay in the room with him. Furthermore, travel cots are easy game to climb out of, and they tip over.

Most parents, once a child has threatened to climb out of his cot, surround the cot with a tumble-area of pillows. But a baby can still come to harm crawling around a strange room while his parents, downstairs, think he is safely asleep in his cot.

Hotels, unless you know or can investigate the layout before committing yourself, can be tricky. Dining rooms and television lounges are seldom within hearing of your room and the baby's crying — hence, the baby-listening device. He might go off to sleep like a top, only to awaken frightened at finding himself alone in a strange room, and try to come looking for you. Moreover, should he climb out of his cot, he could bang his head, twist his neck or back, or whatever.

One hazard is that hotel doors can always be opened from within (as a fire precaution), so it is good idea to place a stairguard on the outside of the closed door. Then if the child does get out of his cot and opens the door, he is at least confined to the room — unless he has learned to climb the stairguard! The stairguard in the doorway is also a good idea for toddlers who have graduated to adult beds. But the only safe solution with no baby-listening service is a babysitter in the room.

I shall never forget lying on the sundeck of a hotel in Tenerife and looking up to see a Spanish maid with a tiny toddler in her arms, on a fifth-storey balcony, a tiny girl who looked very like . . . who was *my* little girl! She had climbed out of her cot for the first time, opened the hotel door and was found, luckily, by a hotel maid wandering along the corridors looking for us. I need say no more.

Cruises

Another way to escape the household drudgery — and even enjoy a floating nursery — is on a cruise. Most ships have well-equipped playrooms with trained nursery nurses on board, and usually children under the age of three travel free (provided the carrycot or travel cot will wedge between the two berths of a two-berth cabin). But be sure that there will be someone aboard willing to babysit. One mother I know got through five novels with a flashlight during a cruise of only five days! It is not much fun to find yourself stuck in your stateroom while everyone else on board has a good time at the fancy dress ball. Most cruise ships do not have a baby-listening service, so it's either you or a babysitter.

Still, there is somewhere to leave the baby or toddler while you and your husband go ashore for sightseeing during the day and a cruise does relieve you of cooking in a most sumptuous and bottom-broadening manner. *Note:* do check carefully the layout of the ship. How many flights of stairs will you and your husband have to hump the carrycot, or the pushchair, or the toddler, up and down from stateroom to nursery, to dining room? Sometimes by booking carefully, you can eliminate several flights.

Travelling with Two Tots

Be it staying for a weekend with friends or going on holiday, travelling becomes twice the trauma with two little bundles of joy. To start with, not many houses have *two* guest rooms these days, and not many guest rooms are big enough for a double bed, a single bed (or mattress), *and* a cot. So unless your friends have children whose room(s) will accommodate another mattress on the floor, or Granny doesn't mind having the toddler on a mattress in her room (not forgetting night feeds, the baby must stay in your room) once your youngest abandons the carrycot, there are far fewer friends and relatives who will be able to accommodate you as a family.

Getting to wherever you are going can have its problems as well, as you juggle the differing needs for meals and sleep of each age group. With a baby in a carrycot, you might set out early in the morning, stop to give him a feed, pop him back into the carrycot and continue driving until the next feed. But with a toddler aboard constantly chattering and, after the first half hour, repeatedly asking how soon you are going to arrive and so possibly keeping the younger child awake . . .

I have friends who swear by recorded stories on cassettes which keep the toddler diverted. If your child is not yet interested in stories, what about nursery rhymes? We started singing — all of us — Ba Ba Black Sheep and Three Blind Mice, over and over again, whenever we went any distance in the car, almost before our toddler could talk, and she loved it. 'More, more' she'd cry until we were almost hoarse. Amazingly enough, it didn't even seem to keep the baby awake. It is best to start just before nap time, or after an early evening tea — the darkness will help to keep them asleep.

Apart from logistical planning, it is an inescapable fact that once you have two children, taking a holiday can suddenly become dramatically more expensive.

Staying in a *self-catering* cottage, caravan, or camping, will hold the cost down, unless you decide to separate the children at night, and therefore, need a bedroom for each of them, i.e. a three-bedroomed cottage. Joining another couple with a child or two of about the same age(s), who could share the room with your children, if there are enough beds or mattresses, or if one or two are still in a travel cot or carrycot, can help to keep the cost down; but count on bedlam for a night or two until they get used to sharing the room.

The good old *farmhouse* bed and breakfast and evening meal routine can solve the problem, if you enquire ahead to find out if there is a bedroom large enough to accommodate all of you. Sometimes farmhouses do have extraordinarily large rooms. If not, paying for two rooms, even at reduced children's or baby's rates, will cost you considerably more (ask about weekly rates).

Hotels, either in this country or abroad, except in Latin countries, rarely have large enough rooms to accommodate families of four, although sometimes you can be pleasantly surprised. Alway ask. What many *do* have are adjoining rooms. This is far more pleasant than the 'small-hour tiptoe' — removing your shoes and jewellery outside your door so that you don't jingle, dropping your clothes in a heap and groping for the bed in the dark without stubbing your toe, and hoping it won't squeak as you climb in so as not to wake the little dears . . . and had you thought of sex?!

Some tour operators give children's discounts without insisting that the children occupy the parents' room. But usually, even in hotels that happily grant reduced rates for young children, the moment you ask for an extra room, any 'free child' offers disappear.

Apart from the expense, there are the safety precautions for the toddler. You might lie down with the children in the hotel room to get them off to sleep, but invariably, one will take much longer to drop off, keeping the other awake, and you run twice the risk of waking one or the other as you try to slip out for dinner. The answer is to hire a babysitter to sit in the room with the children, unless you trust a hotel's baby patrol or baby-listening service. In this case it is wise to keep the stairguard on the *outside* of the hotel room door, to keep the toddler in the room should he wake up and open the door.

Even on *cruises* which, according to the brochures, allow children under three to travel free, the moment you enquire about a four-berth cabin, up goes the cost. The rate for the two adults in a four-berth cabin is within a few pounds of the cost for two, two-berth cabins — and they won't let you use the second cabin for the *free* children. So the 'free child' offers melt away, unless it is one child fitted into a two-berth cabin, probably in a carrycot, as few double cabins will also accommodate a cot. Obviously, there are many companies, but you will need not only to read the fine print, but to enquire carefully about how the *free* child offers actually work.

As I write this, we have just had a holiday in a rented villa in Spain with our two children, aged two and four. The flight from a nearby airport took only two-and-a-half hours, during which the youngest was enthralled by a bag full of new toys. As Spaniards are much more relaxed than the British about having children underfoot in restaurants, we found that having lunches out in beachside restaurants, and in town at the marvellous cafeterias (no waiting for service), solved some of the catering problems. We swooned over the splendid view of the sea from our verandah at breakfast and supper, and the children adored the huge, fenced-in garden, and the beach.

The cost of this holiday for the *four* of us was about the same as our holiday the previous year to America — for the *two* of us! As we were only able to find a babysitter for one evening though, it was lonely. Once the chldren were in bed, we had only one another to talk to and a few books to read after we'd watched the glorious sunset. And when we got back home, I had to admit that I felt that it would have been very nice to have a holiday from the holiday — away from the kids . . .

To Take Them or Leave Them?

If you can possibly arrange it, leave them. Once a baby is weaned, why not enjoy a real holiday — away from *your* job? After all, you deserve your own small measure of leisure!

Child psychologists sometimes talk about the irreparable damage to young children which is caused by being separated from their parents. But I often wonder about the irreparable damage done to young children by tired, miserable, frustrated and short-tempered parents, which must be equally harmful to both parents and children. How much better for the children to have more happy, relaxed parents, refreshed after a break, than to have parents who are short of patience and constantly screeching in anger.

A fortnight away from a child is not going to wreak much anguish on the child, surely, especially if he knows the person he is to be left with and enjoys that person's company. It simply means finding the right person and taking the time to let the child become happy and secure with that person; it is well worth the bother for a blessed break from domestic drudgery and childcare.

These days not many of us are lucky enough to have grandparents who live close by, or who are fit enough to look after a young child for a fortnight. Little wonder! It is a daunting enough job for a young and fit woman. But if you can manage to leave the child, even for the occasional weekend, the relief is immense.

If there is no one that you know locally, who is already acquainted with the baby, there are agencies in London who will supply a nanny or granny-type person to look after your child(ren) while you go away. Of course, it does cost money, but you might be surprised at the cost of taking the baby with you. Even for a baby under two, a hotel will charge you for the cot, milk, possibly hot water, and for food from the buffet if he eats any, and babysitters in hotels are not cheap! Over the age of two, and you will have to pay a not-very-reduced air fare as well. Of course, you might take a nanny, granny or younger sister along with you to look after the baby, but that really is rather extravagant when you start counting up the cost of an extra fare, extra room, etc.

One solution, if there really is no one with whom you can leave the baby, is to combine forces with another family having a baby of about the same age. It's wise to check what the other child's nap pattern is before setting out, or you might find yourself hemmed in to do all the daytime baby-sitting; for instance if you have a heavy sleeper, and the other couple's toddler has given up naps altogether. Still, if they do the night-duty sometimes while you and your spouse whoop it up, it might be a fair exchange. It is best to explore how the tiny people's schedules mesh before setting out.

Personally, I take the hard line — that a holiday with small children is not really a holiday for mum: it is just child-minding transplanted to a different, and possibly less convenient and more hazardous, environment. But a change, shared with dad, is better than no change at all, or so I keep telling myself.

Getting away — really getting away, from the children — does help. The only trouble is that some parents wish that they didn't have to come back!

20. Conclusion

You might well wonder, in the words of that rueful phrase, 'Had I known then, what I know now', would I still have had children?

It is not an easy question to answer. From reading the previous chapters, you might be forgiven for leaping to the conclusion that I loathe motherhood and only see the negative side of it. I have made very little effort to lard into these chapters the joys and the love that I feel for my own children. This is so over-abundantly done in every other baby book I have ever read that I felt that the other side of the coin needed inspecting. So the preceding chapters are the rock and bones reality of child-rearing, with the emotion pretty well strained out.

Having experienced what I have, and knowing what I know now, would I do it again? On dark days, when the seven years of intensive motherhood before the youngest will start at school seem to stretch to infinity, or whenever I sit down with the brochures to try to find a holiday, that is really a holiday for me, that we can afford with the added expense of two small semi-civilized people, the answer is a resounding NO.

But now that they are here, rant and complain as I do, I couldn't possibly wish them not here. Noisy, devilish, obstinate and mischievous as they are, the next moment they are beguilingly charming, flirting with our affections in a thoroughly disarming manner. As I wrote about our younger child:

> In some ways our youngest was an even easier baby than our daughter. He took to solid food like a baby bird, his little mouth wide open whenever a spoon appeared, and when it came time, he accepted the bottle within a week.
>
> It had been with very mixed feelings that I set out to wean him. Breast-feeding is such a close and tender time, and as we had decided to have only two children, I knew that this was the last time

that I would ever suckle a baby. I was almost disappointed that he took to the bottle so readily.

But with the foresight and foreknowledge that I hope this book has provided, deciding to have children again would not be such an easy decision. When I was contemplating having a second child, it was a very different world. Were I having to make that decision today, the odds would weigh far more heavily on the negative side.

For instance, would I deliberately choose to bring children into a world where the possibility of nuclear devastation looms quite as frighteningly as it has for the past few years? Or into a world where the threat of starvation looms large if we do not develop other sources of food (and energy) by the end of the century, when our children will be reaching adulthood? Or into a world where unemployment begins to look like a way of life as Western economies reorganize themselves, pushed out of world markets for manufactured goods by low wage-paying Third World countries? Or if you really want to worry about the future, into a world in which the polar ice cap may be melting, reducing our cultivable land? Or into a world which might enter another ice age in as short a time-span as ten years? (See *Ice* by Fred Hoyle, published by Hutchinson).

On a more personal level, the most often expressed motives for having children don't really stand up to much rational examination:

1) *It's expected of us by parents and grandparents.*

So what? We live in a very different world in which, for the first time, we have the choice of whether or not to breed.

2) *To carry on the 'line'.*

What earthly difference does it make when you are dead whether or not your 'line' continues, and who can say how your progeny might turn out?

3) *To preserve the species.*

Unfortunately, mankind is already reproducing so over-abundantly that people are now starving in many parts of the world.

4) *To prove your feminity/virility.*

Surely there are other ways?

5) *Because it's an 'experience' you wouldn't like to miss.*

Keep in mind that 'having a baby' is only the beginning, the very beginning, and the experience of rearing a family goes on for twenty years or so!

6) *Because you love children and like being with children.*

This is the only genuinely justifiable motive that I can think of, although social workers might say that there are already plenty of children needing your love and caring, without you producing your own.

As I said in the Introduction, deciding upon whether or not you want to become a mother is diabolically difficult from the 'before' side of the decision, unless you have a lot of experience with young children upon which to base your decision. Otherwise, despite this book, it is still impossible to know how you will react actually to becoming a mother. I only hope that if you do decide to become a parent that you now feel better prepared for what having a family will mean.

As you ponder over the uncertainties of our world, asking yourself if you want your children to have to struggle against all of the odds set out above, you might wonder if the Western world might not have sorted itself out by the time that our children have grown up. Certainly, every generation has felt that the world was becoming a worse and worse place in which to live, so why let it bother us?

It is just as easy to say, with all of these odds *against* the world being a very pleasant place in which to live by the time that our children grow up (if, indeed, they have the chance to grow up!) why bother having children at all? Why not just enjoy life, live life for today and let tomorrow take care of itself?

Or on the contrary, you may feel that whether or not the world is apt to self-destruct, that you would prefer to have had children, than not to have had them, and later find that the world has somehow muddled through.

I'm afraid I have no answers to these impossibly difficult questions. You must decide for yourself. In any case, many women go on having babies every day, I suspect, without giving it much thought! More's the pity.

If *you* do decide to become a parent, I only hope that you will feel ready for it.

Bibliography

Archard, Merry, *Kids Bloody Kids,* George Allen & Unwin, 1972.

Azrin, N. & R. Fox, *Toilet Training in Less Than A Day,* Pan Books, 1977.

Barber, Virginia & Merrill Maguire Skaggs, *The Mother Person,* Severn House, 1977.

Boston Women's Health Collective, *Ourselves & Our Children,* Penguin, 1981.

Dowrick, Stephanie & Sibyl Grundberg edits., *Why Children?* Women's Press, 1980.

Hann, Judith, *A Working Parent's Guide, What About the Children?'* Bodley Head.

Haycroft, Anna, *Natural Baby Food,* Fontana, 1980.

Hull, Sylvia, *Cooking for a Baby,* Penguin, 1979.

Kitzinger, Sheila, *Women As Mothers,* Fontana, 1978.

Kitzinger, Sheila, *Research from Women's Experiences of Episiotomies,* National Childbirth Trust.

Lennane, Jean & John, *Hard Labour,* Victor Gollancz, 1977.

Oakley, Ann, *From Here to Maternity,* Pelican, 1981.

Manley and Ree, *The Piccolo Book of Games for Journeys,* Pan, 1972.

Nicholson, Joyce, *The Heartache of Motherhood,* Sheldon, 1983.

Peck, Ellen, *The Baby Trap,* edit. by Robert Chartham, Heinrich Hanau, 1973.

Salk, Dr. Lee, *Preparing for Parenthood,* Robert Hale, 1974.

Wallace, Karen, *The Pan Picnic Guide,* Pan, 1983.

Whitehorn, Katharine, *How to Survive Children,* Eyre Methuen, 1974.

Useful Addresses

National Childbirth Trust
2 Queensborough Terrace
LONDON W2 3TB

National Housewives Register
245 Warwick Road,
SOLIHULL
West Midlands BG2 7AH

Pre-School Playgroups Association
Alford House
Aveline Street
LONDON SE11 5DH

Index

adjustments, 14–17, 20, 47–49, 51–52, 57–60, 77, 92, 96–97, 101–108, 110–111, 117, 126–129

age gaps, 115–120

aggression, 39–40, 118, 148, 152–153

ante-natal care, 72–74

babies' personalities, 43–46

baby battering, 38–42

baby clothes/equipment, 29–31, 55–57

babysitting, 27, 32, 36, 41, 50, 52, 59, 60–63, 66, 68–69, 93, 106, 110, 113, 125, 128–129, 150, 159–163, 165–167

baby carrier, 105, 111

bathing, 14, 23, 93, 98, 100–101, 109, 118, 152

birthday parties, 71

'bonding', 57

boredom, 18, 108, 110–112, 123

bouncing chair, 19, 44, 47, 110

breaks, 20, 41, 53-54, 56, 60–61, 106, 141–143, 145, 166–167

Caesarean birth, 17, 82, 87, 95

carrycots (prams), 30, 33, 47, 65, 80, 94, 101–102, 103–104, 105–106, 111–113, 115, 123, 125, 127, 146, 155–165

carseats, 27, 33, 64, 112–113, 123–124, 137, 157, 160

childbirth
emotional reactions, 84–89
help after, 57–59, 94, 150, 159
labour, 17, 73–74, 84, 87, 95, 107
Leboyer method of, 84
preparation for, 49–51, 68, 78–82, 150
recovery after, 17, 49–50, 52, 81, 86, 95–96, 100–102, 107–108, 110, 113, 117, 119, 123, 147, 150, 152, 156

childminders, 14, 16–24, 33, 59, 61–63, 97, 111, 144, 166

cooking, 78–79, 92–94, 97–98, 100, 145, 160–161, 163

cosmetics, 80

costs, 26–35, 115, 118, 129, 154, 160, 164, 166, 168

cots, 30, 104, 112, 157–159, 162–163, 165

crawling, 20, 50, 75, 108–110, 112, 115–116, 121–125, 133, 138, 152, 154, 157, 159–161

cruises, 156, 163, 165

crying, 13–15, 29, 38–40, 44, 46, 49, 54, 65, 74, 81, 85, 88, 96, 101–103, 111, 115, 119, 125, 127, 147–148, 151,

157 – 158, 160 – 162
day nurseries, 14, 16, 21
depression, 18, 54, 94, 128, 142, 145

episiotomy, 52, 74, 96, 107 – 108, 128
escape, 20, 33 – 34, 41 – 42, 53, 60 – 61, 106, 113, 123, 129, 141, 143, 145, 166 – 167
experts, 74
extended families, 20, 68
fathers/fatherhood, 13 – 16, 22 – 23, 32, 47 – 49, 58 – 59, 79, 81, 90 – 94, 106, 121, 123 – 124, 127, 139, 142, 145, 149 – 150, 154, 156, 159
feeding
    bottle, 14, 16, 49, 56, 59, 82, 93, 118, 155 – 156
    bottles, 81 – 82
    breast, 14, 16, 29, 47 – 48, 50 – 53, 55 – 56, 65, 68, 77, 80 – 82, 85, 88, 93, 96, 100 – 103, 114, 155 – 156, 168
    breast pumps, 81
    breast versus bottle, 80 – 81
    by fathers, 81
    costs, 29
    'mixed', 24, 81, 82
    night, 20, 29, 49, 51 – 52, 55, 59, 81, 95 – 96, 101 – 102, 107 – 110, 116 – 117, 119, 148, 150 – 152, 155 – 156, 163
    'real' food, 50, 56, 134 – 135
    routine, 44, 77, 92, 96 – 97, 98 – 101, 111, 114, 116, 118, 148, 155
    solid food, 29, 69, 101, 108 – 110, 133, 135, 151, 155 – 156
    themselves, 135 – 137
    twins, 118

unpredictability of, 44
weaning, 24, 82, 110 – 112, 133, 155 – 156, 166, 168
frustration, 20, 38 – 41, 52 – 53, 123, 135, 139 – 142

Gingerbread, 37
grannies, 28, 32 – 33, 54, 57 – 63, 79, 129, 139, 147, 150, 163, 166
guilt, 19, 39, 96, 107, 118, 127, 141, 144, 151 – 152

hair, 80, 124, 128
hiccups, 14, 29, 93
holidays, 33, 36 – 37, 61 112, 119, 155 – 167
hospital/maternity homes, 16 – 17, 56, 72 – 74, 88, 95, 98, 128, 147
housework, 21 – 23, 57, 59, 61, 77, 79 – 80, 83, 90, 94, 98, 100, 102, 117, 124, 144 – 145, 160
housing, 26, 29

journeys, 112, 124, 138, 157, 163-164
joys, 18 – 19, 27, 35, 47, 77, 84 – 89, 96, 104 – 105, 110, 126 – 127, 133, 168 – 169

labour, 17, 84, 87, 95, 107, 128, 147
Leboyer method, 84
loneliness, 37, 77, 101, 111, 117, 119, 147, 165

marriage, 19, 47, 92, 142
maternity clothes, 31, 51, 80
morale, 54, 85, 91 – 92, 98, 112, 126 – 129, 143 – 144
mothers/motherhood
    job description, 18, 92
    roles, 14, 16, 19 – 21

stay-at-home, 19, 21–22, 102, 126, 140
mother-and-baby/toddler groups, 68, 114, 123, 125, 129, 141
music, 43–45

nannies/childminders, 14, 16–24, 33, 59, 61–63, 97, 111, 144, 166
nappies, 30, 35, 47–48, 54, 56–57, 65, 70, 92–93, 97–98, 100, 102, 115, 117–118, 126, 146, 152–153, 155–156, 158
National Childbirth Trust, 68, 107–108, 114, 143
National Housewives Register, 68–69, 143
night waking, 15, 45–46, 97
nuclear families, 20
nursery school, 27, 69–70, 110, 112, 117, 139, 150–151, 154

obedience, 46, 51, 124–25, 133
outings, 32–33, 36–37, 51, 53, 63–65, 69, 81, 93, 105–06, 111–113, 118, 123–125, 129, 134, 137–138, 153–154
    competition, 69–71
    effects on lifestyle, 14, 47–49, 63–69, 90–93
    preparation for, 49–51, 68, 78, 82
Parents Anonymous, 42
Parents magazine, study by, 41
'paternity' leave, 16, 57, 79, 90–91
playgroups, 36, 69–70, 110, 112, 117, 139, 150, 154
playpens, 30, 115, 122–123
pocket money, 26, 36, 51
pouches, carrying, 56, 104–105, 112–113
prams, *see* carrycots

preparation, 49–51, 68, 78–82
private education, 28
punishment, 50–51, 152–153
pushchairs, 31, 39–40, 65, 104, 112–113, 118, 123, 125, 127, 134, 137–138, 146, 154, 158, 160, 163

regression, 117, 119, 147, 152–153
relationships with
    friends, 41, 52–54, 63–71, 112–113, 128, 159, *see* also social life
    husband, 47–49, 51–54, 106, 117, 123
    medical profession, 72–74
    relatives, 54–63, 159, 163, *see* grannies
    strangers, 71–74
safety, 15–16, 50, 115–116, 119, 121–123, 133–134, 138, 145, 153–154, 159, 160–162, 165
sanity, 20, 23, 141–142
self-catering holidays, 33, 160–161, 164–165
self-esteem, 143–45, *see* morale
sex, 37, 51–52, 107–108, 110, 128, 165
shoes, 50
shopping, 23, 41, 59, 61, 63, 78–79, 81–82, 93–94, 100–104, 118, 124, 128, 133, 153–154
single parenthood, 35–37
sitting up, 30–31, 46, 104, 112, 119, 133, 152, 154
sleep, 17, 57, 77, 80–81, 87–88, 92–95, 97–98, 100–102, 107, 109–110, 117–118, 149
sleeping (baby), 44, 59, 69, 97, 104, 109, 111–112, 119, 123, 128, 133, 156, 160, 167
social life, 32, 36–37, 41, 52–54, 63–71, 101, 105–106,

112–114, 117–119, 123, 125, 128, 141–142, 157, 160–161, 163, 166
stairguards, 121, 159-162, 165
State benefits, 20, 29, 30, 34–35, 127
Sunday Times, The, study by, 143
sweets, 50–51, 56, 134

talking, 20, 45, 65, 119, 139–145, 151, 164
temper tantrums, 39–40, 45, 119, 148
tension, 41–42, 106, 122–123, 133, 142, 151
tiredness, 21, 23, 49, 51–52, 60, 77–78, 81, 83, 85–86, 88, 91, 94–98, 102, 106–108, 110–111, 117–119, 148, 151
toilet training, 19, 117, 119, 136–137, 148, 158
toys, 36, 40, 45, 110, 115, 118,

122, 124, 126, 134, 136, 147, 152–153, 158–159, 165
tranquillizers, 41, 142
travel cots, 125, 157–159, 162–164
travelling, 119, 155–167
twins, 118

walking, 20, 31, 50, 115–117, 119, 121, 133–138, 160–161
Which magazine, study by, 26–28
working mothers, 14–16, 18–25, 35, 111, 143
  criticism of, 21, 24
  decision to return, 20, 24, 118
  full-time, 21, 142–143
  guilt of, 19
  maternity leave, 20
  need for escape, 18, 54, 92, 127, 142–144
  part-time, 21–22